This Book Belongs To

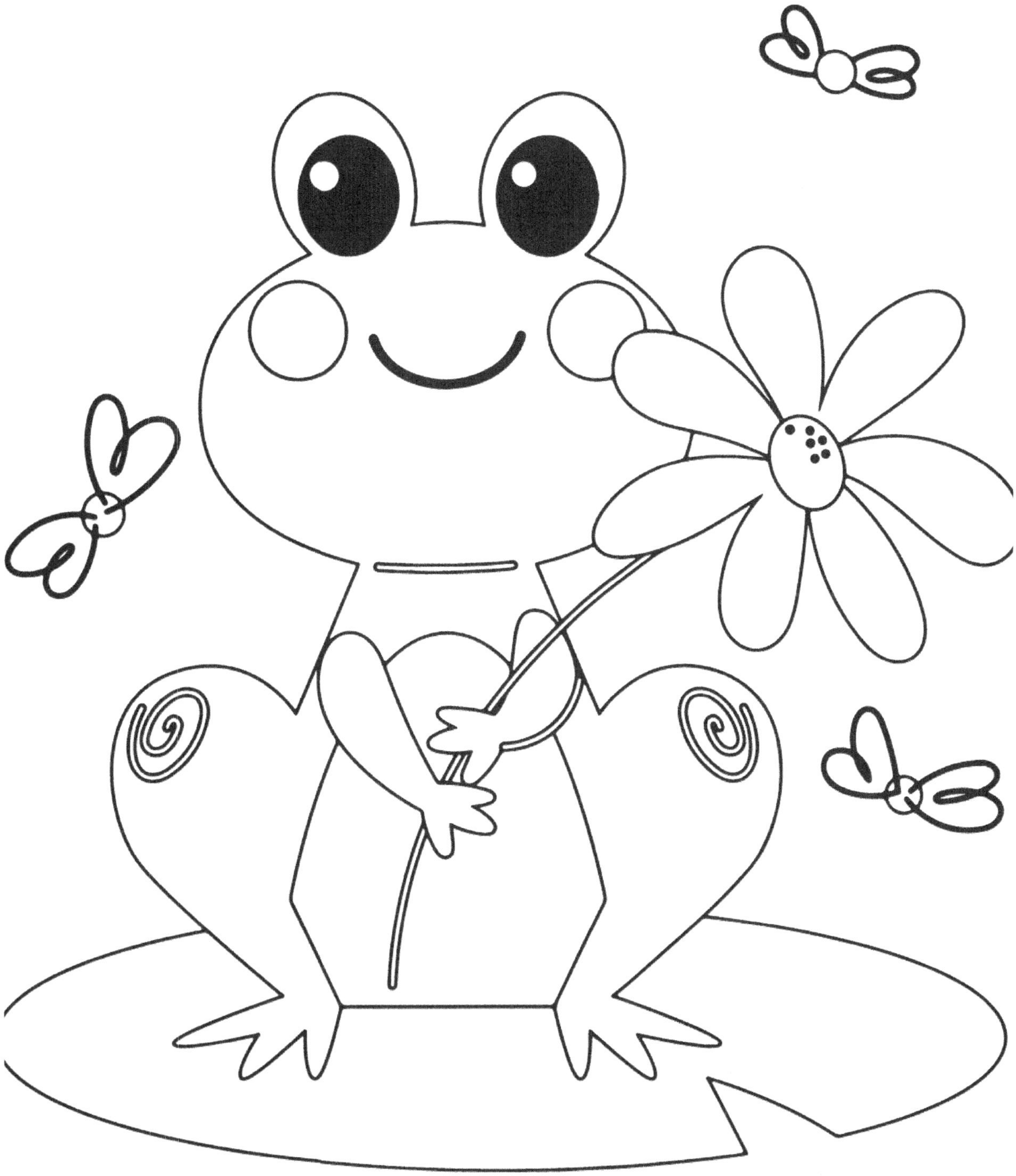

COLOR TEST

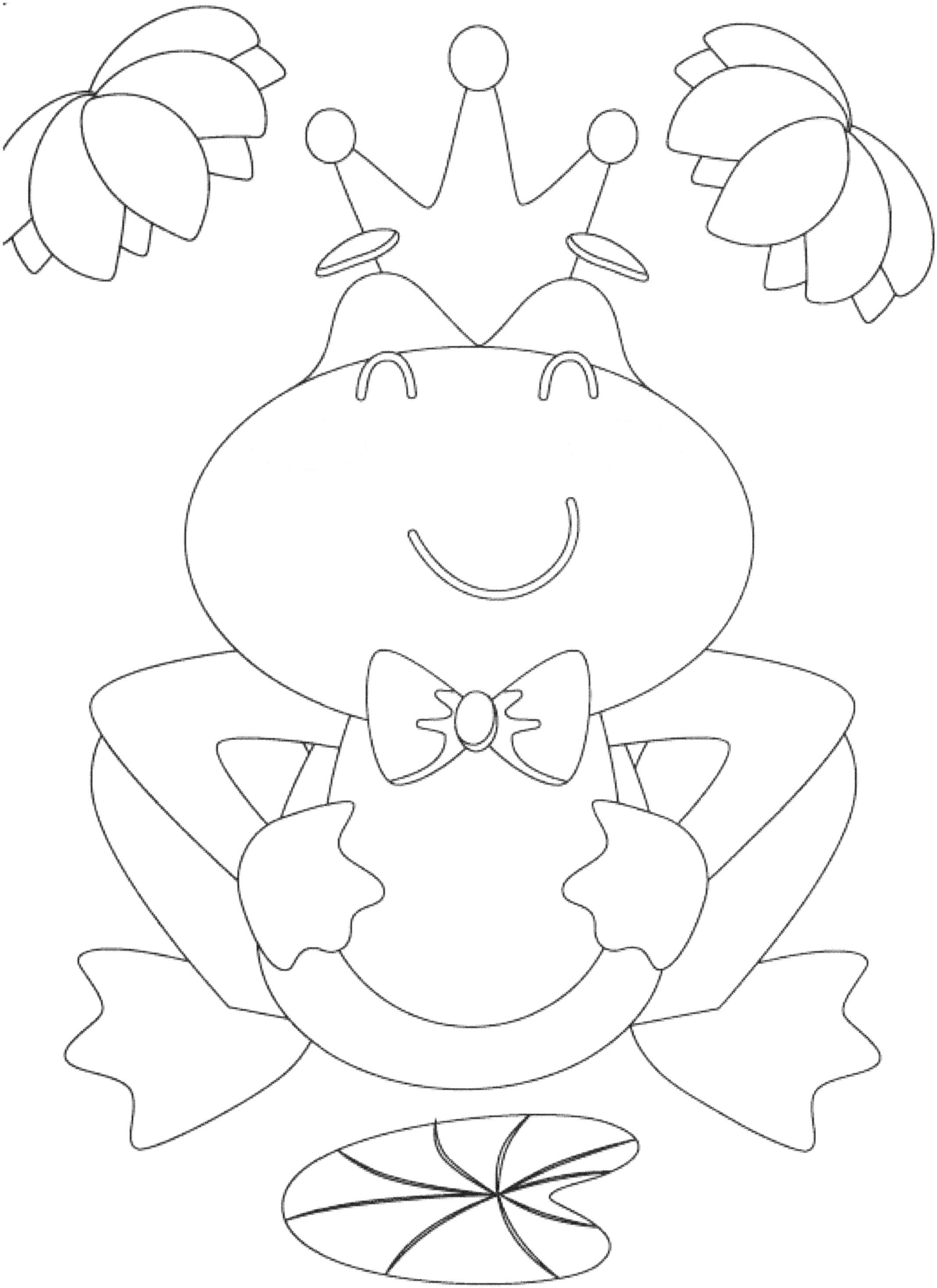

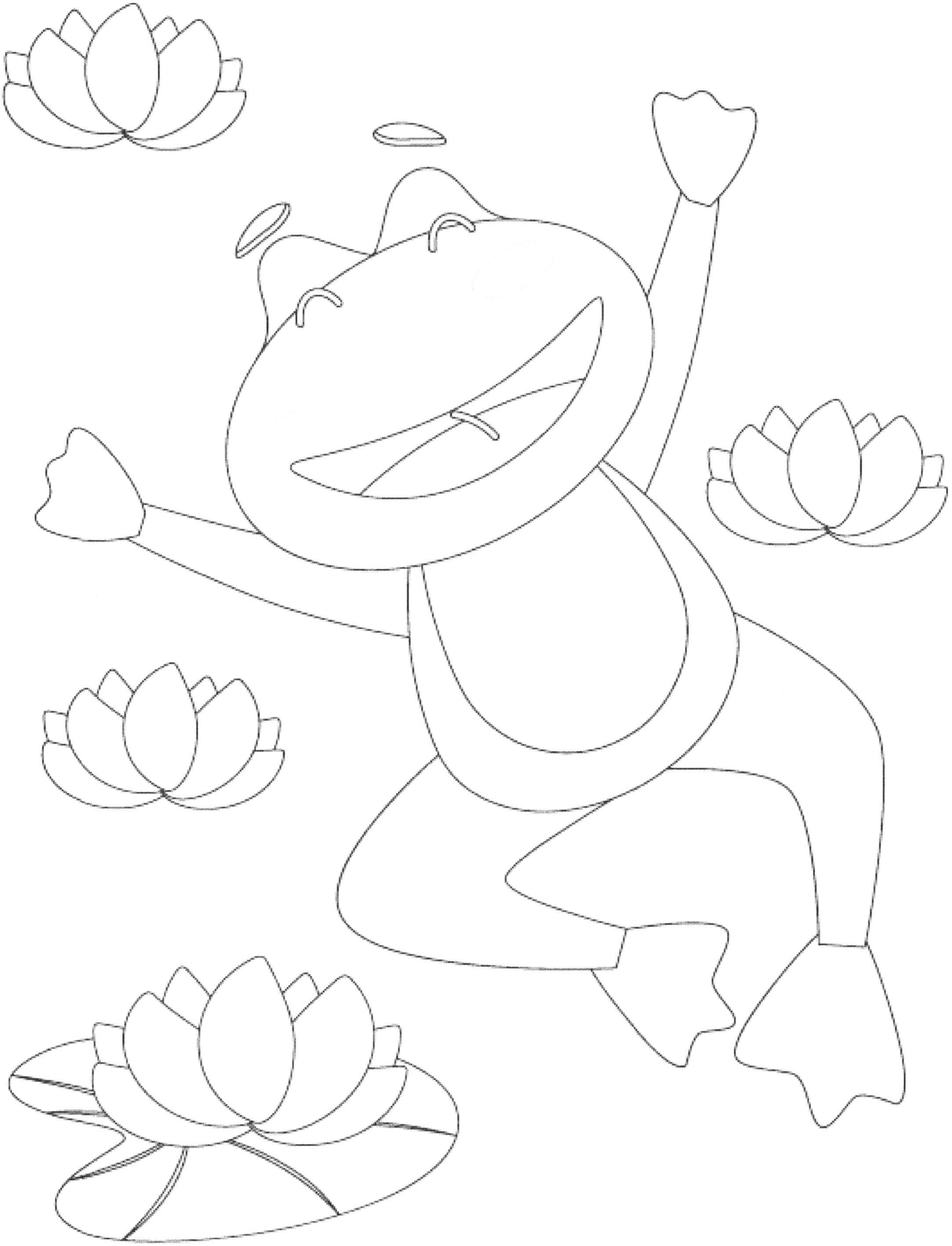

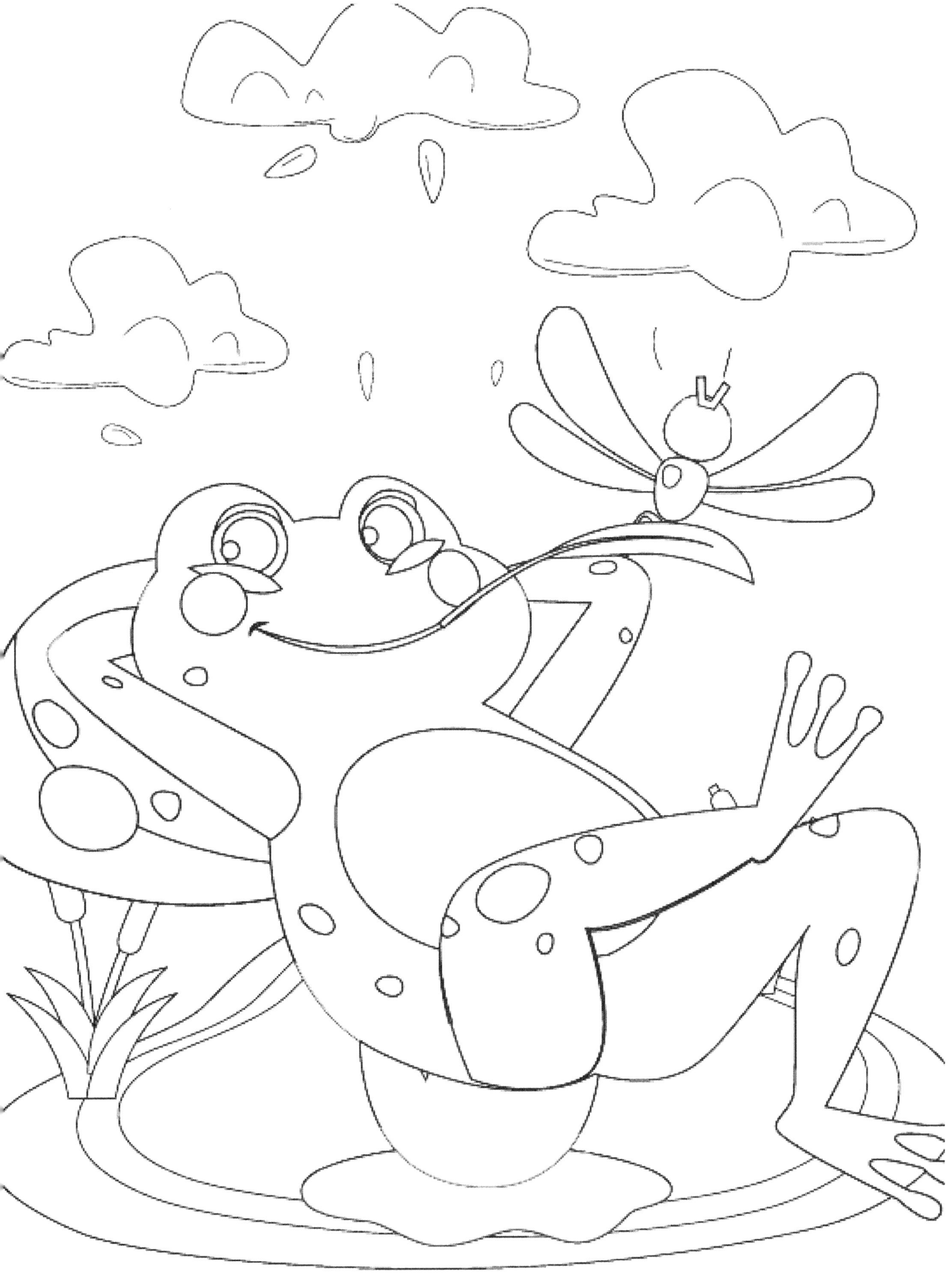

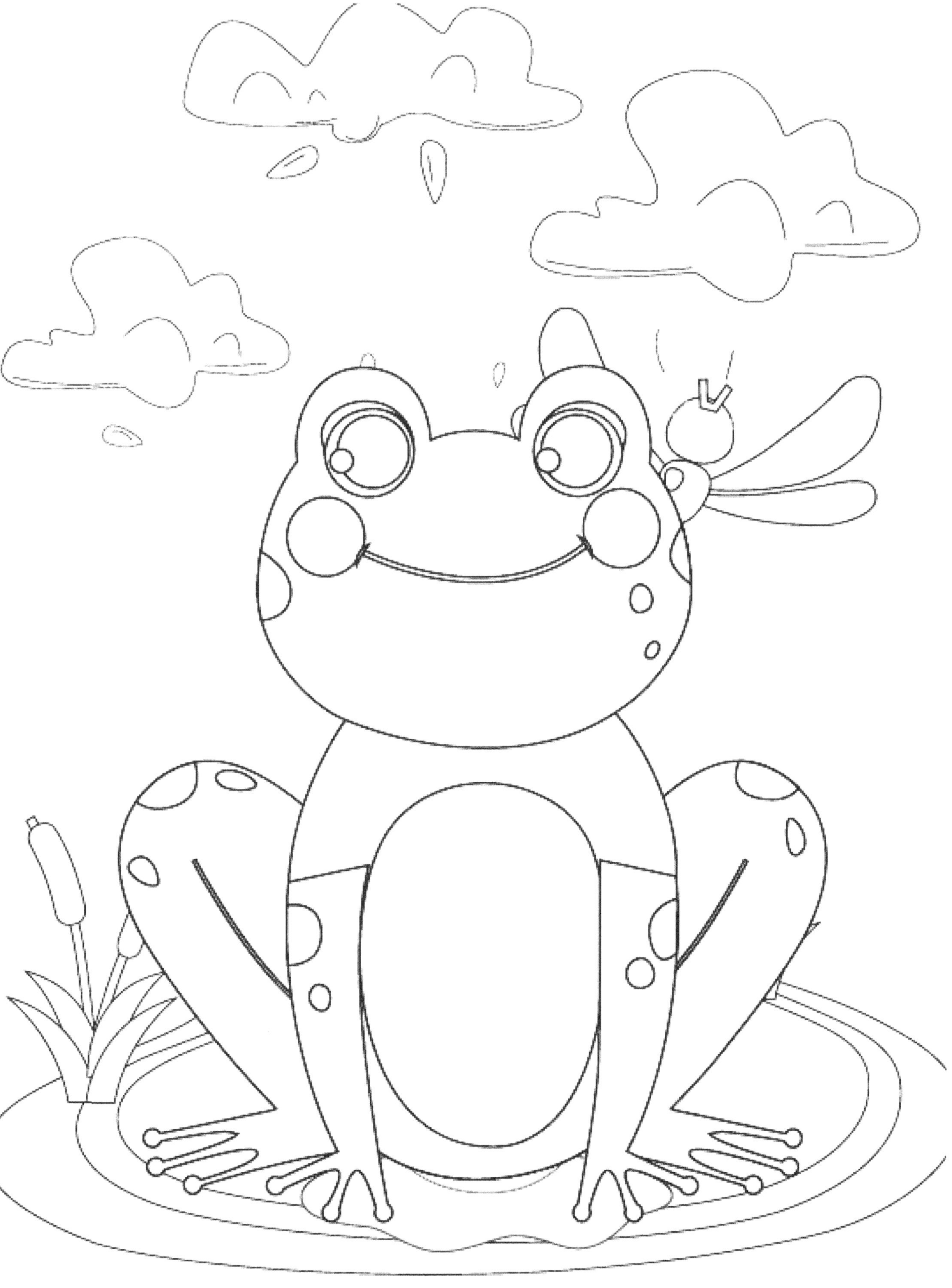

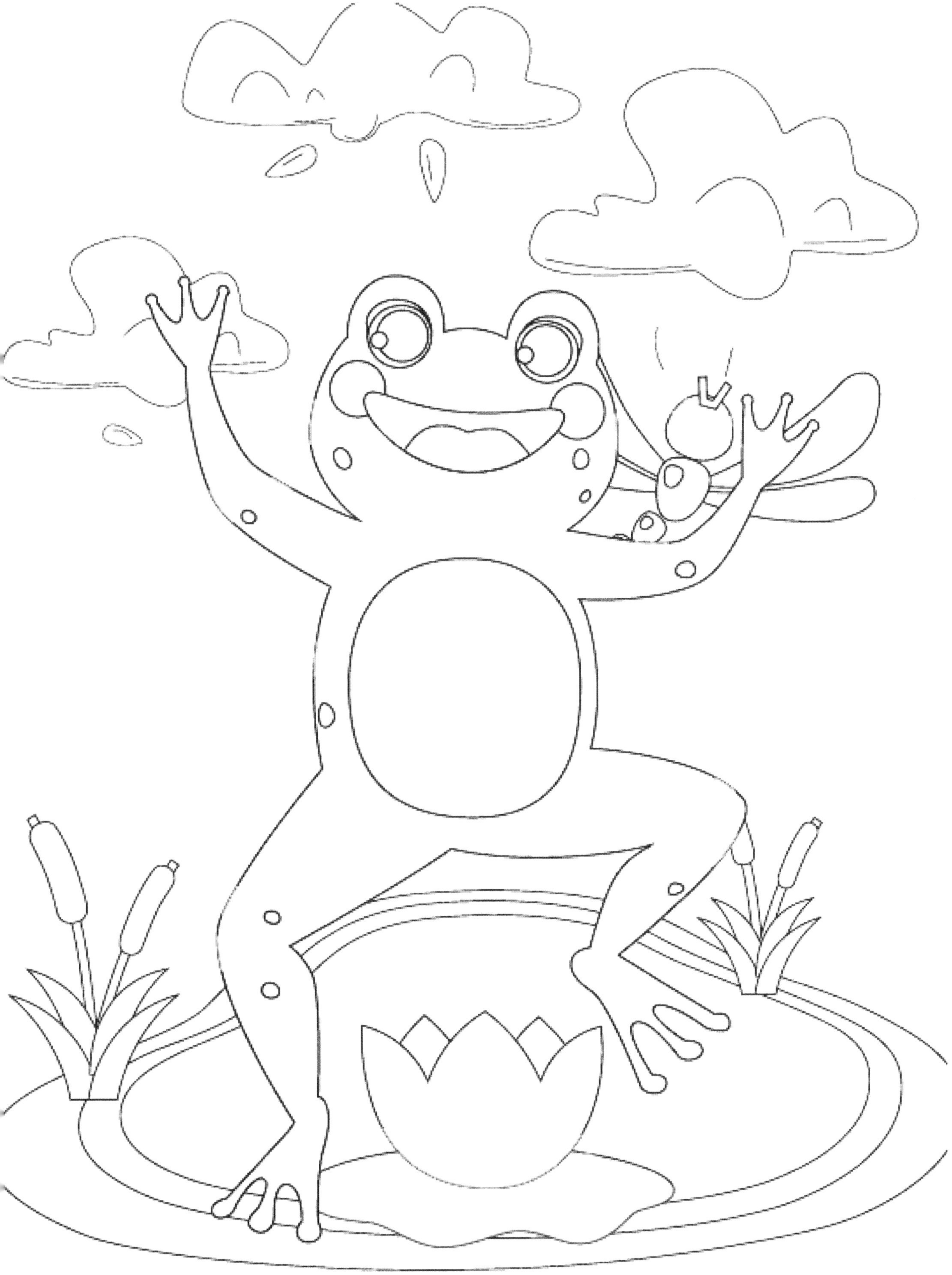

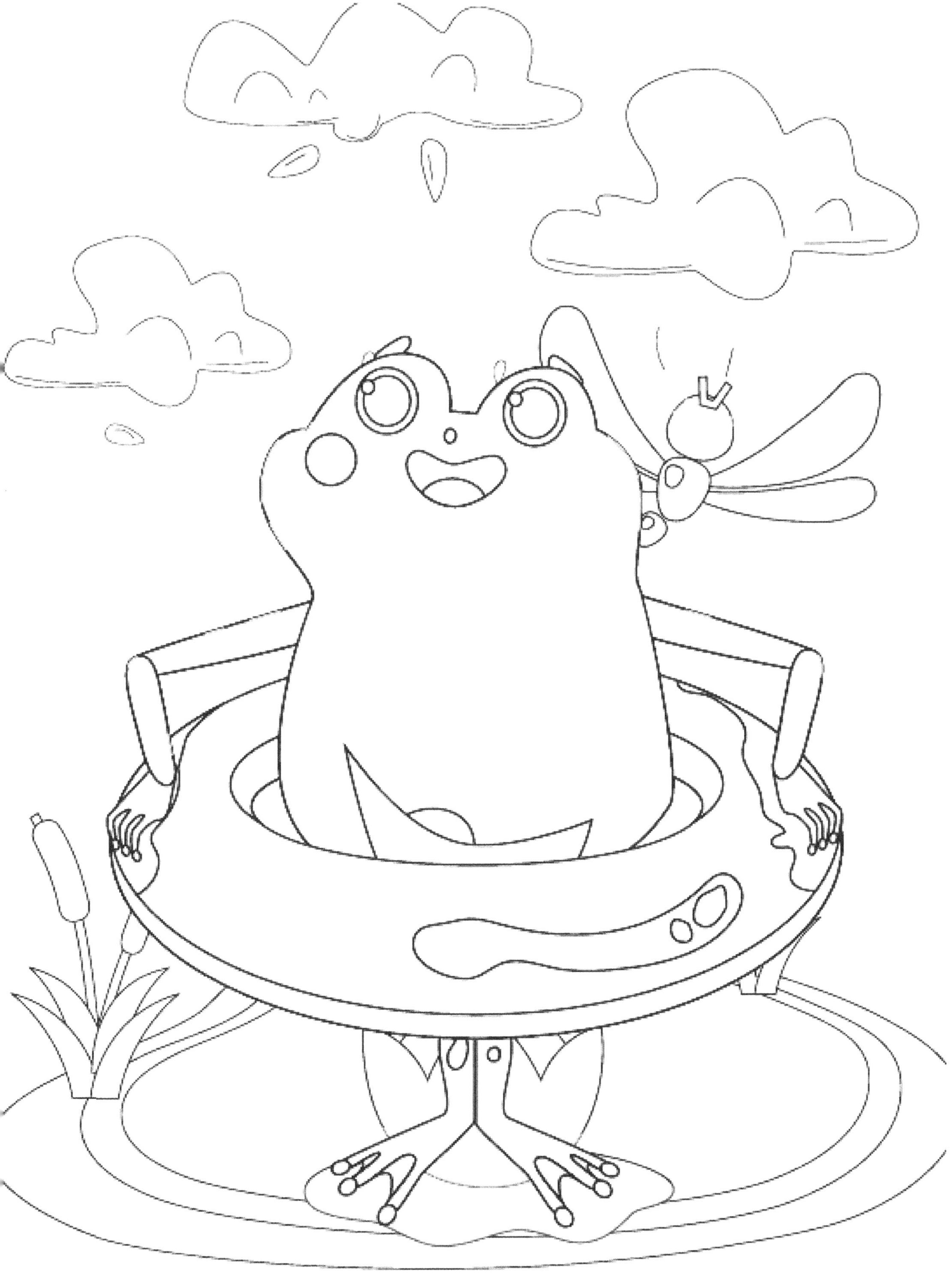

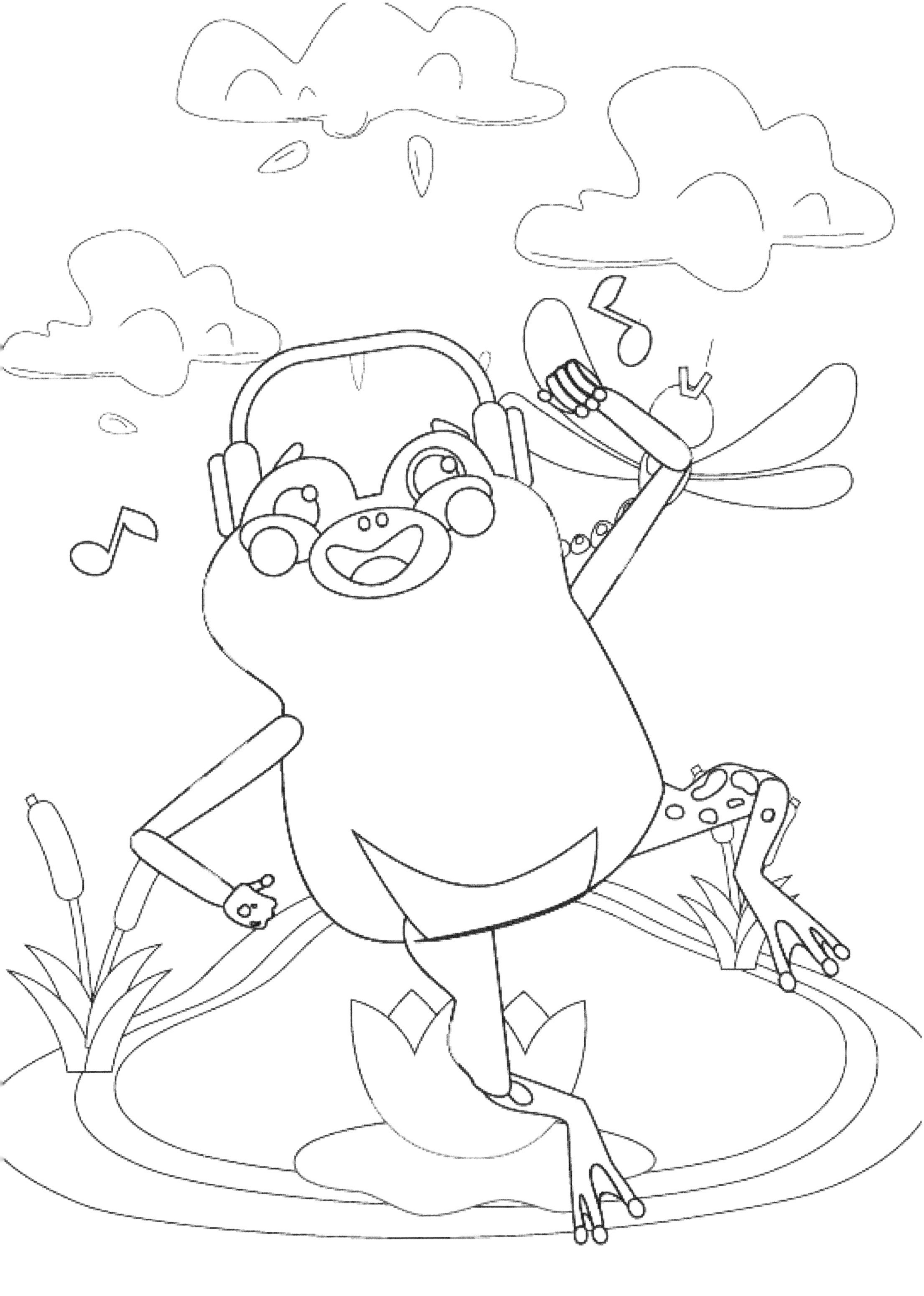

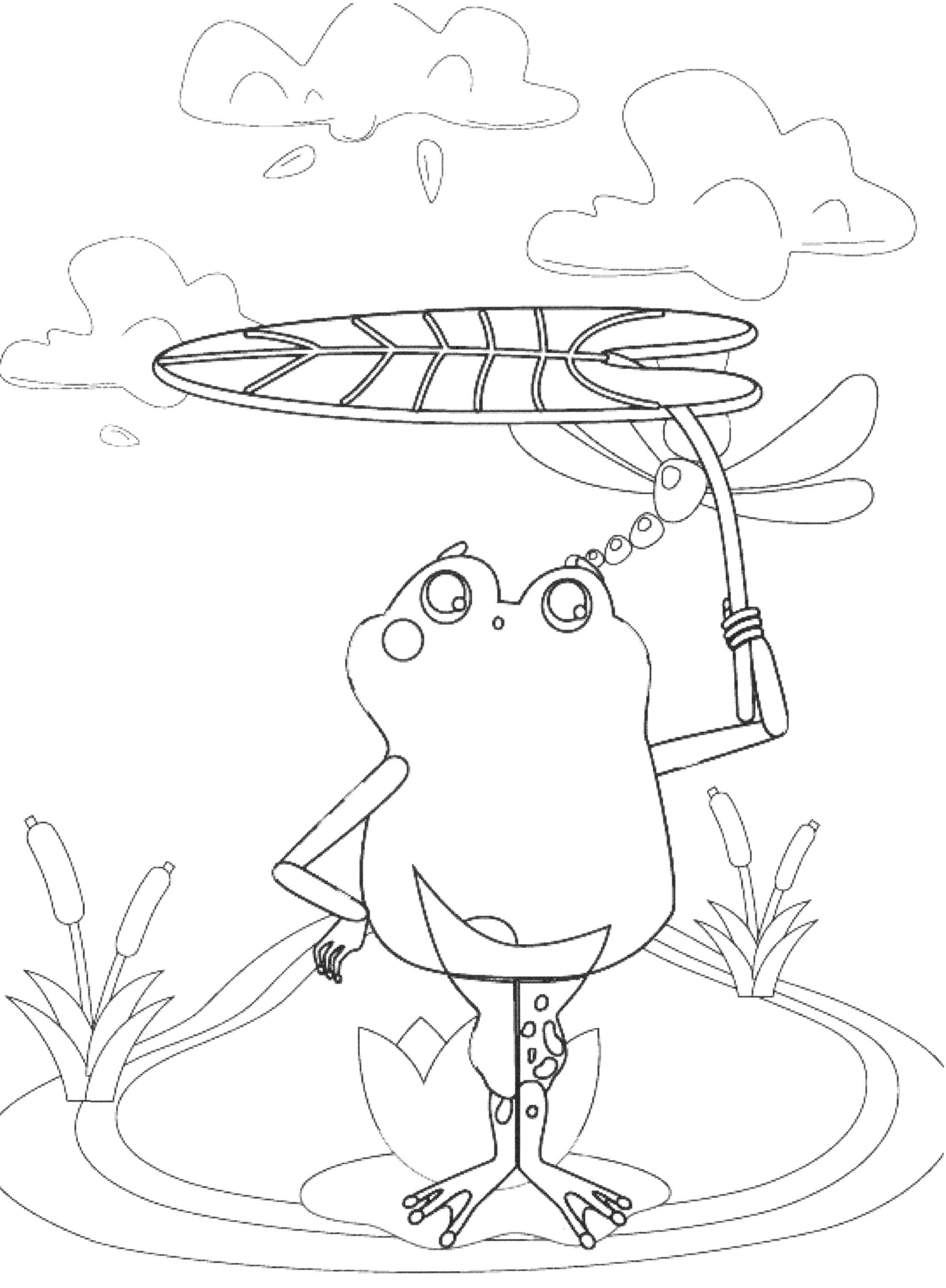

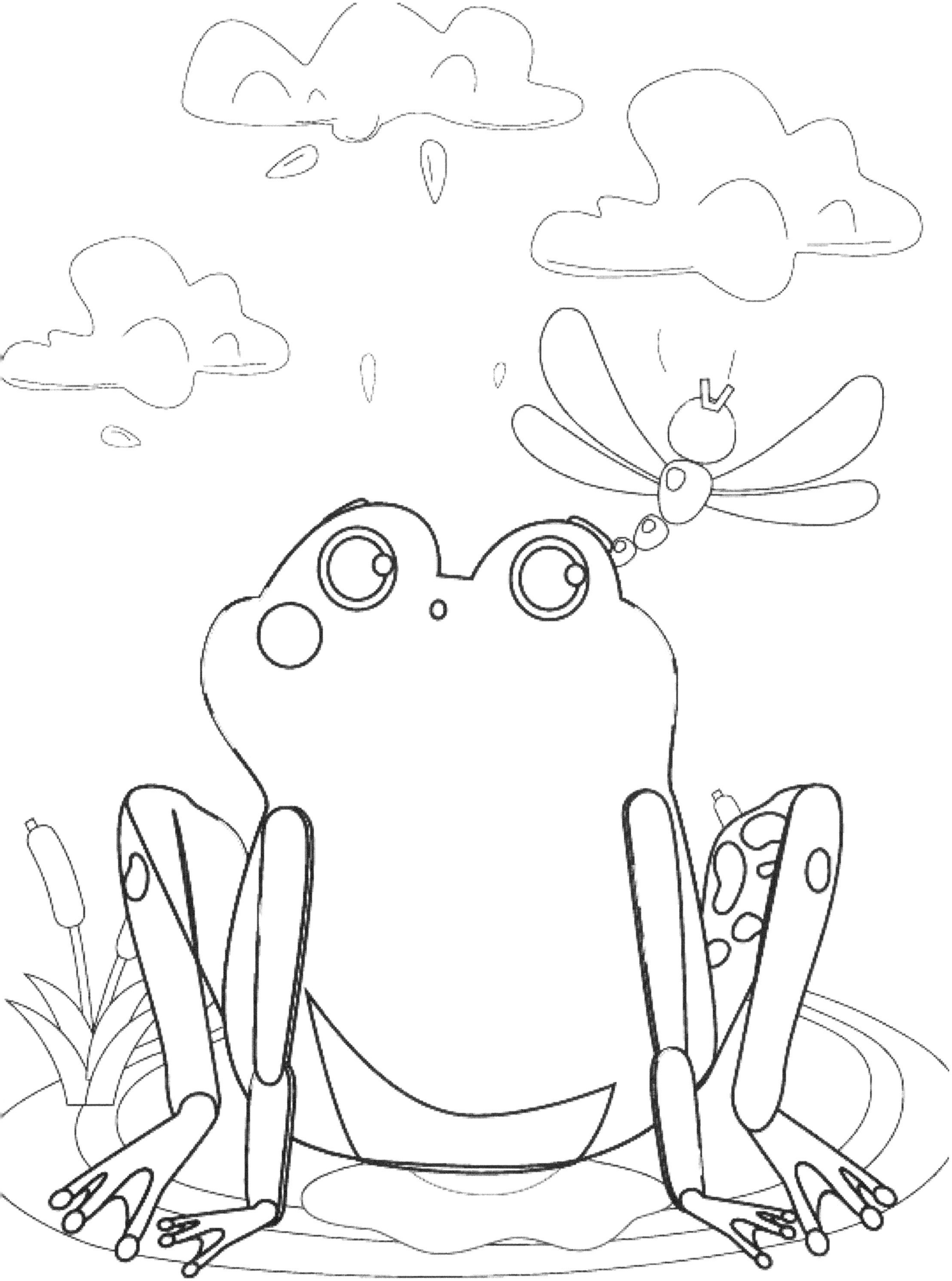

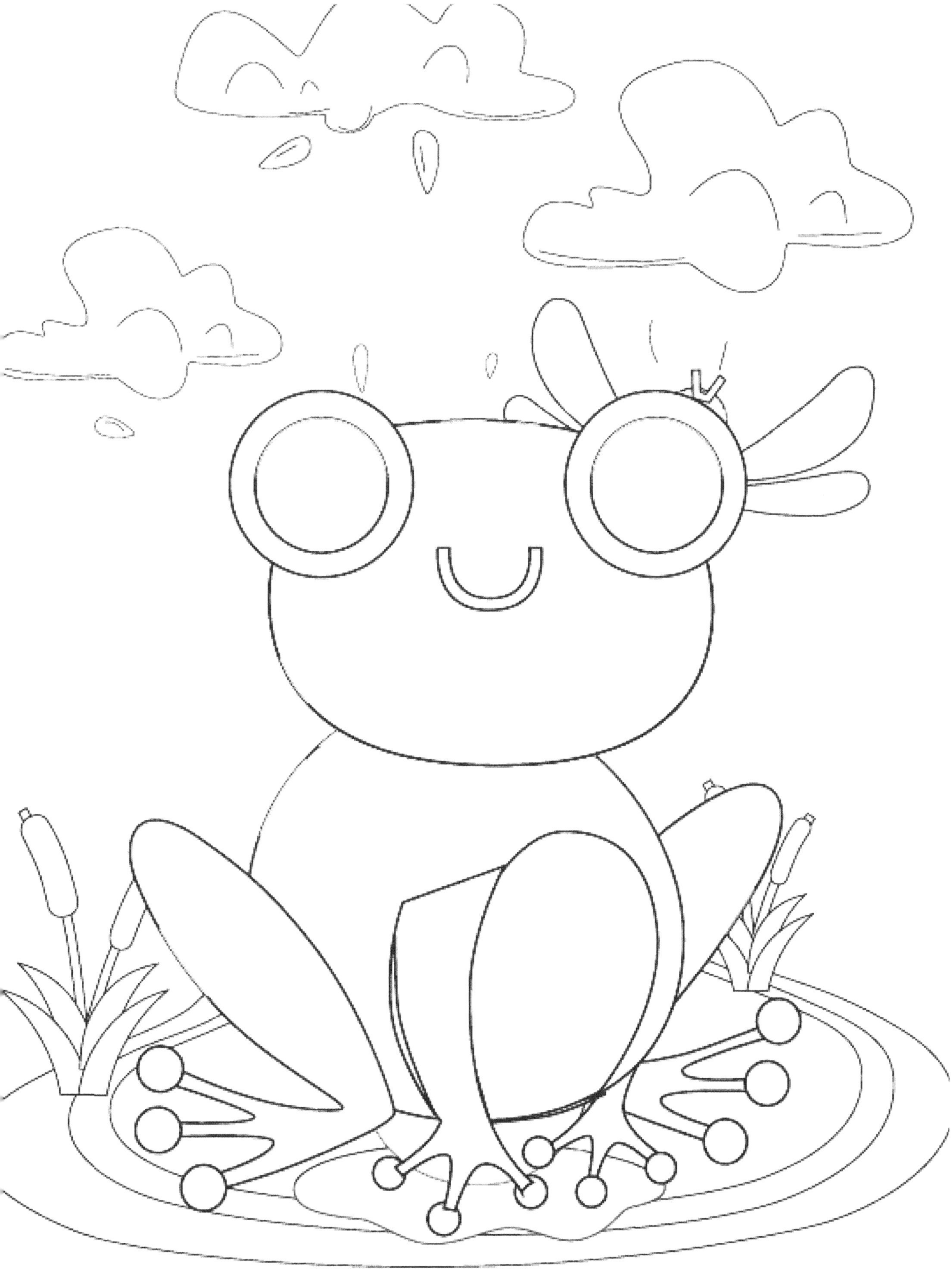

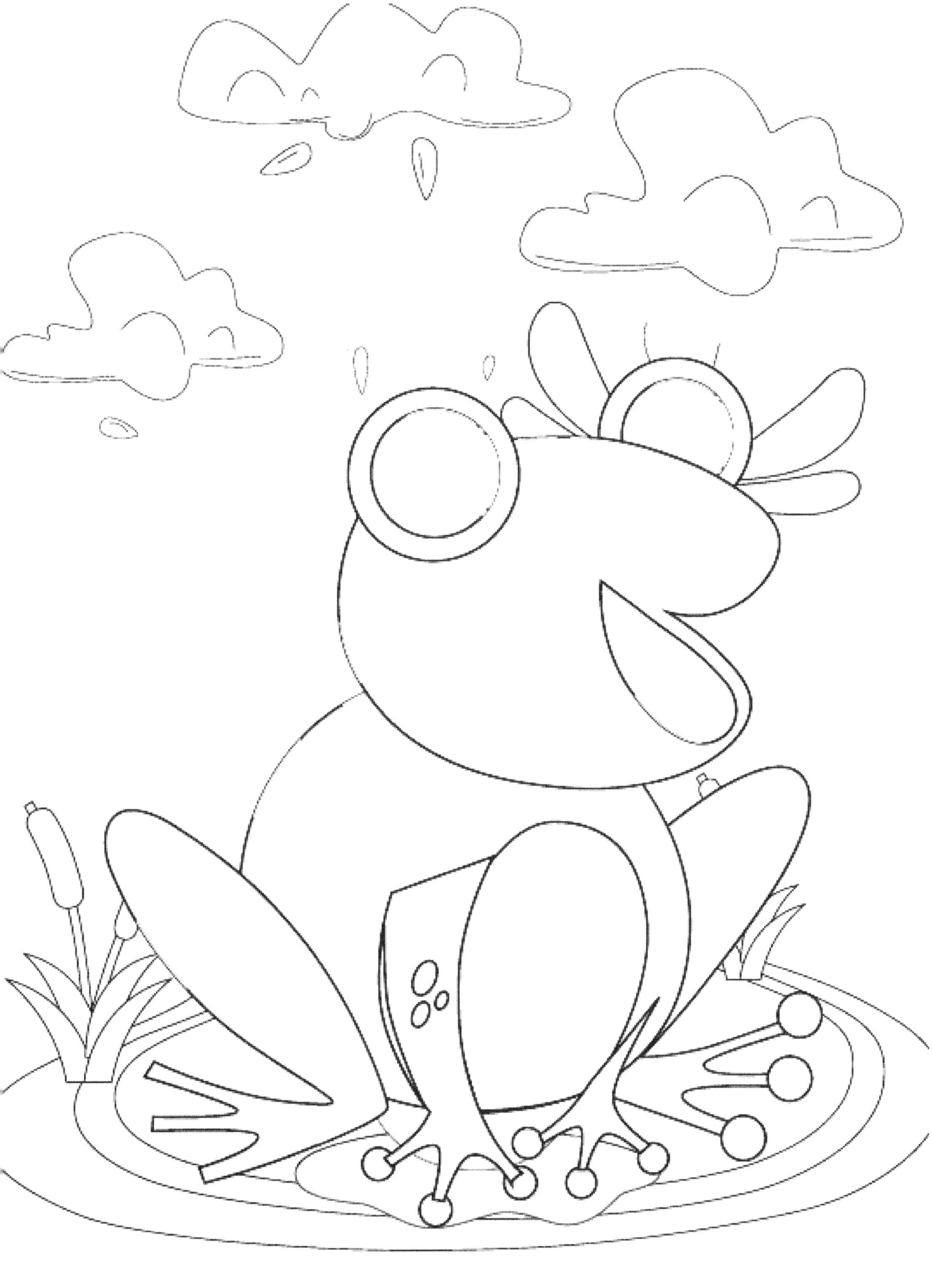

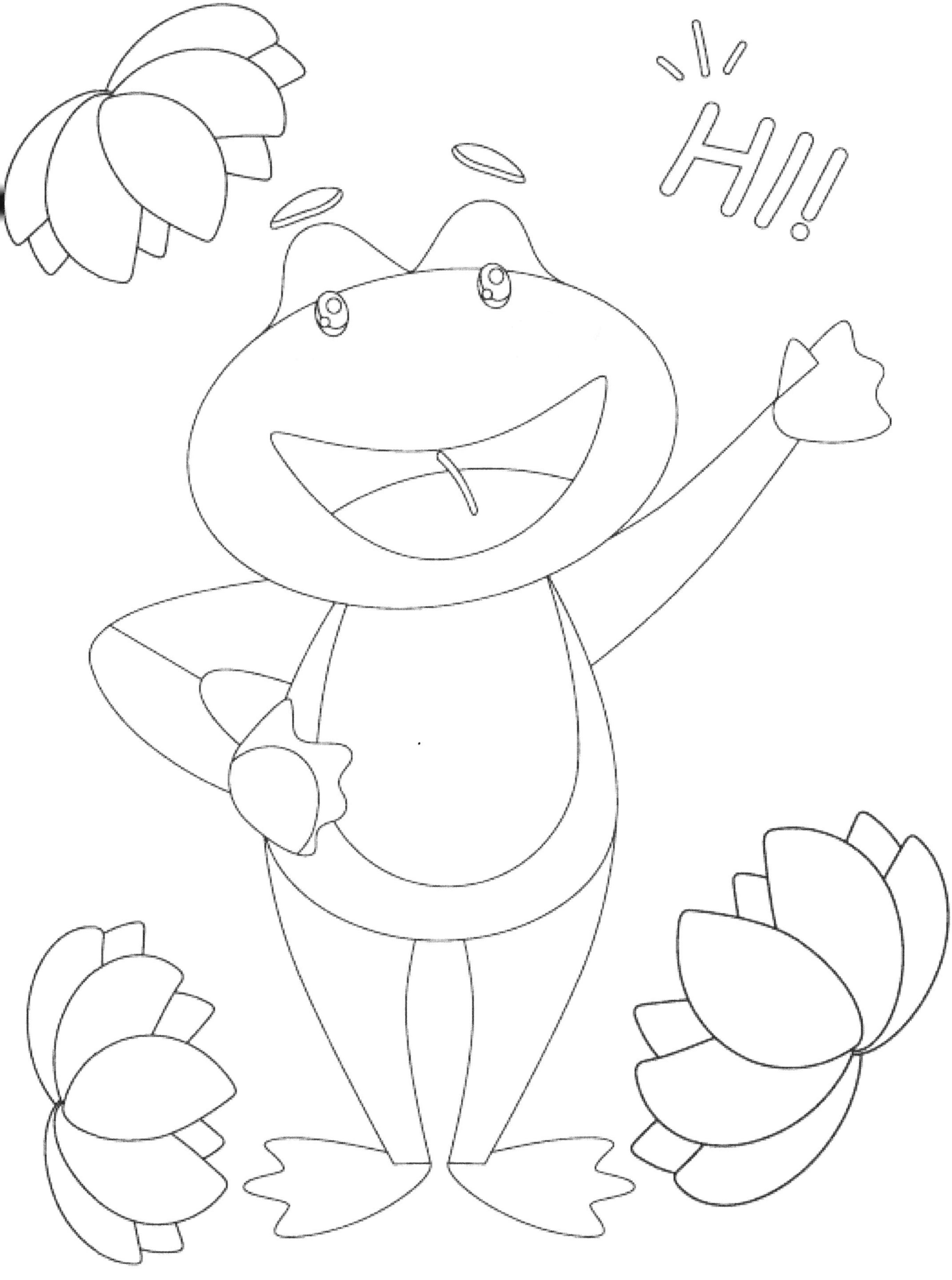
HI!

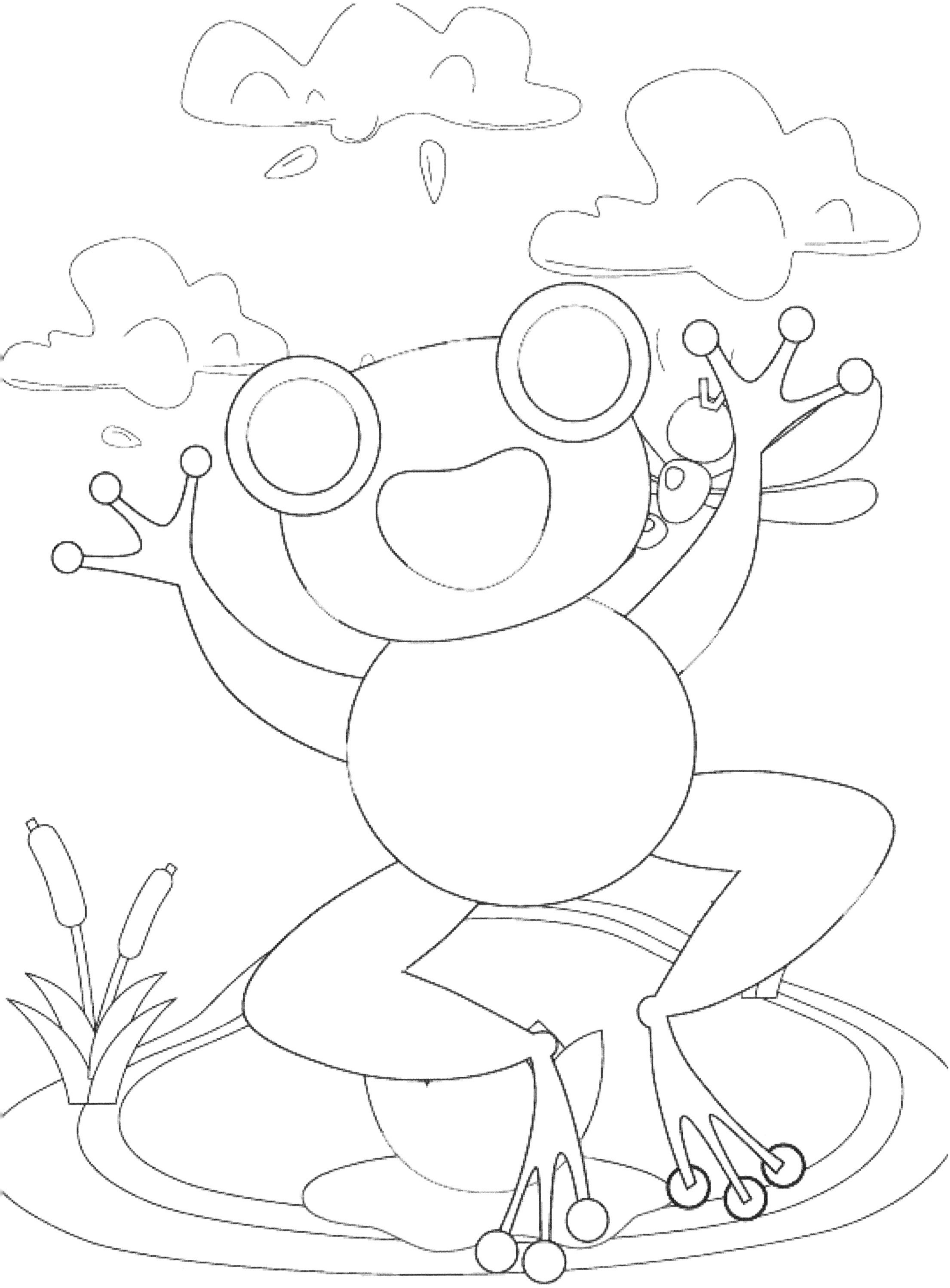

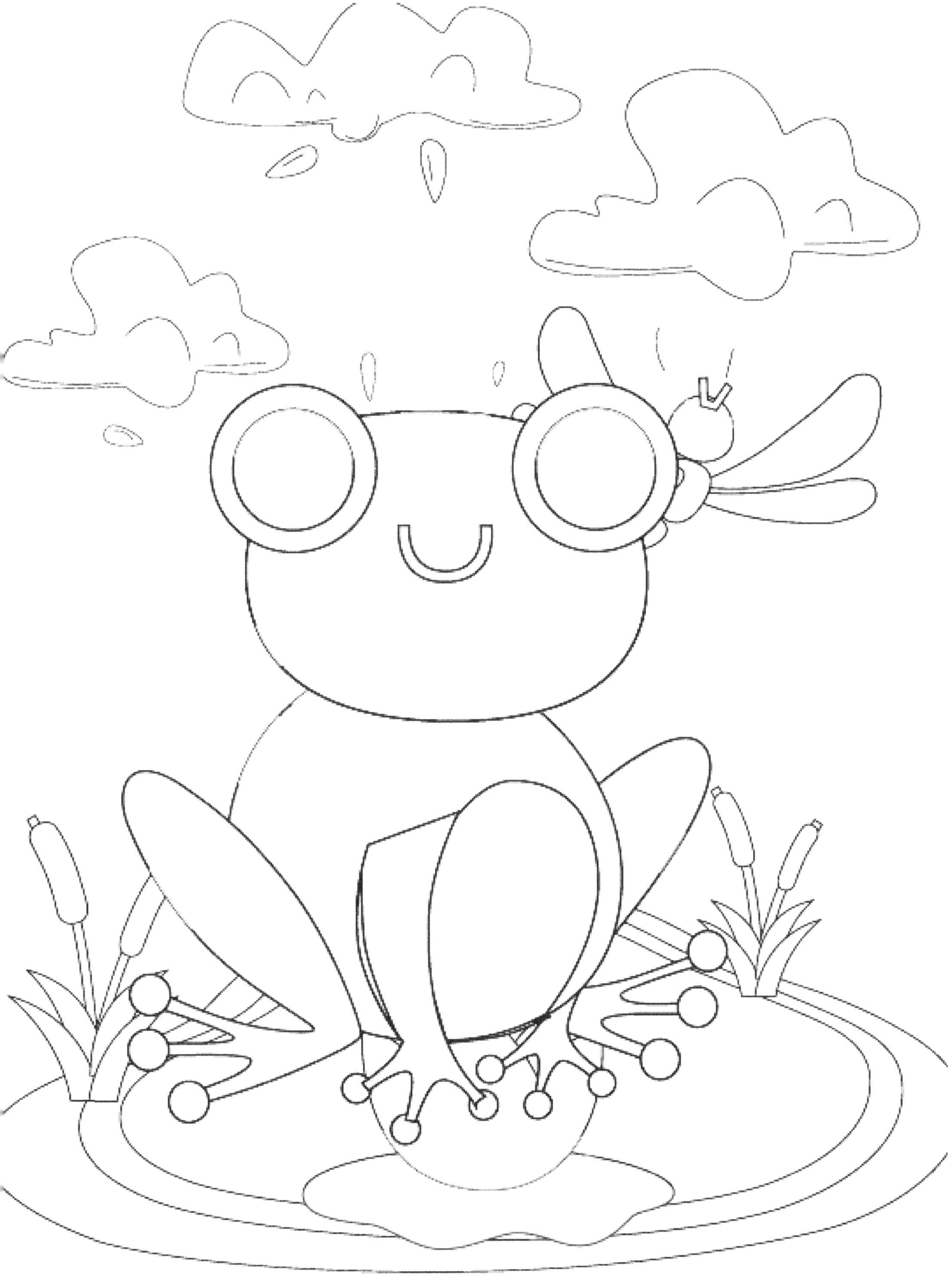

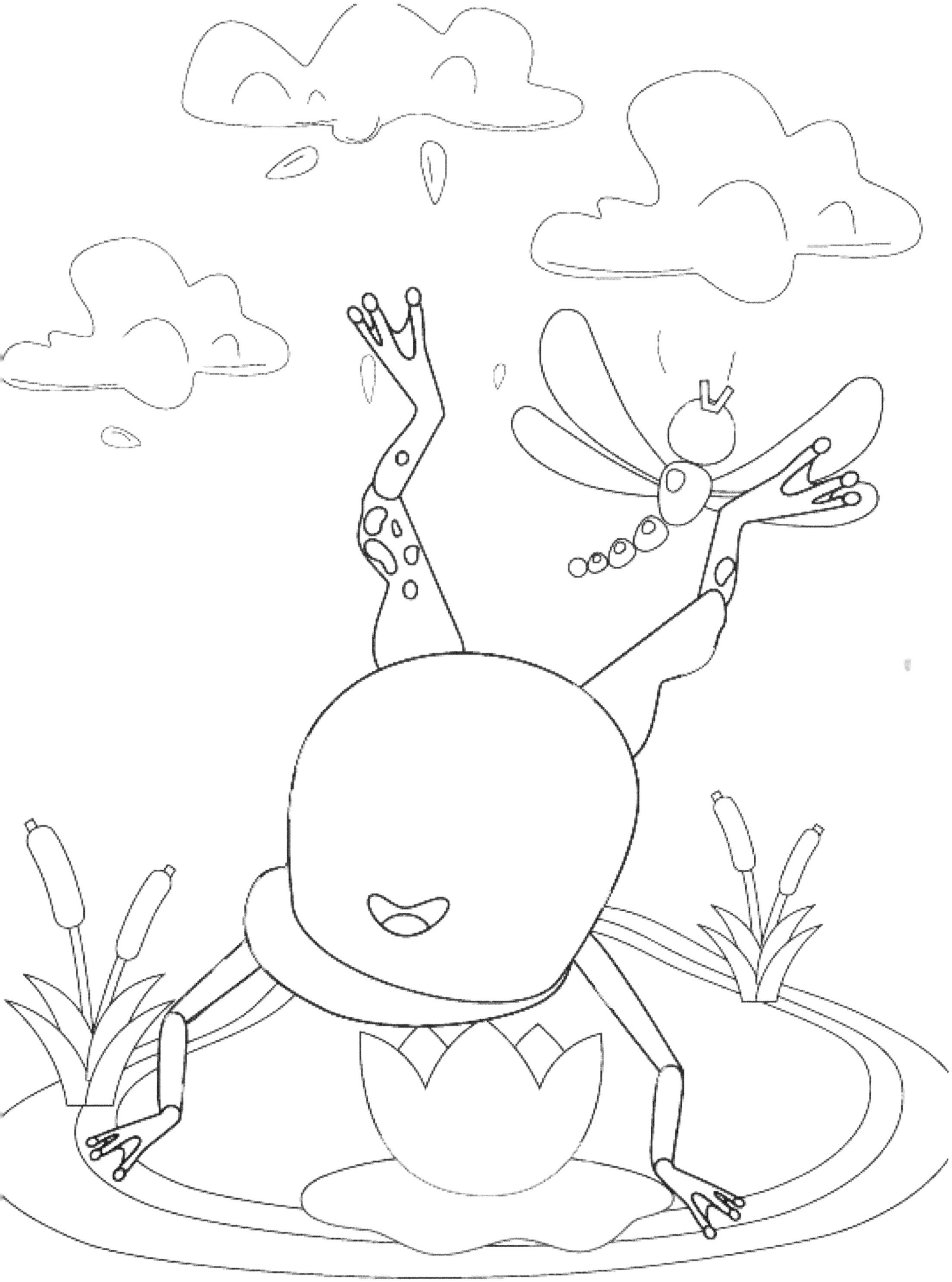

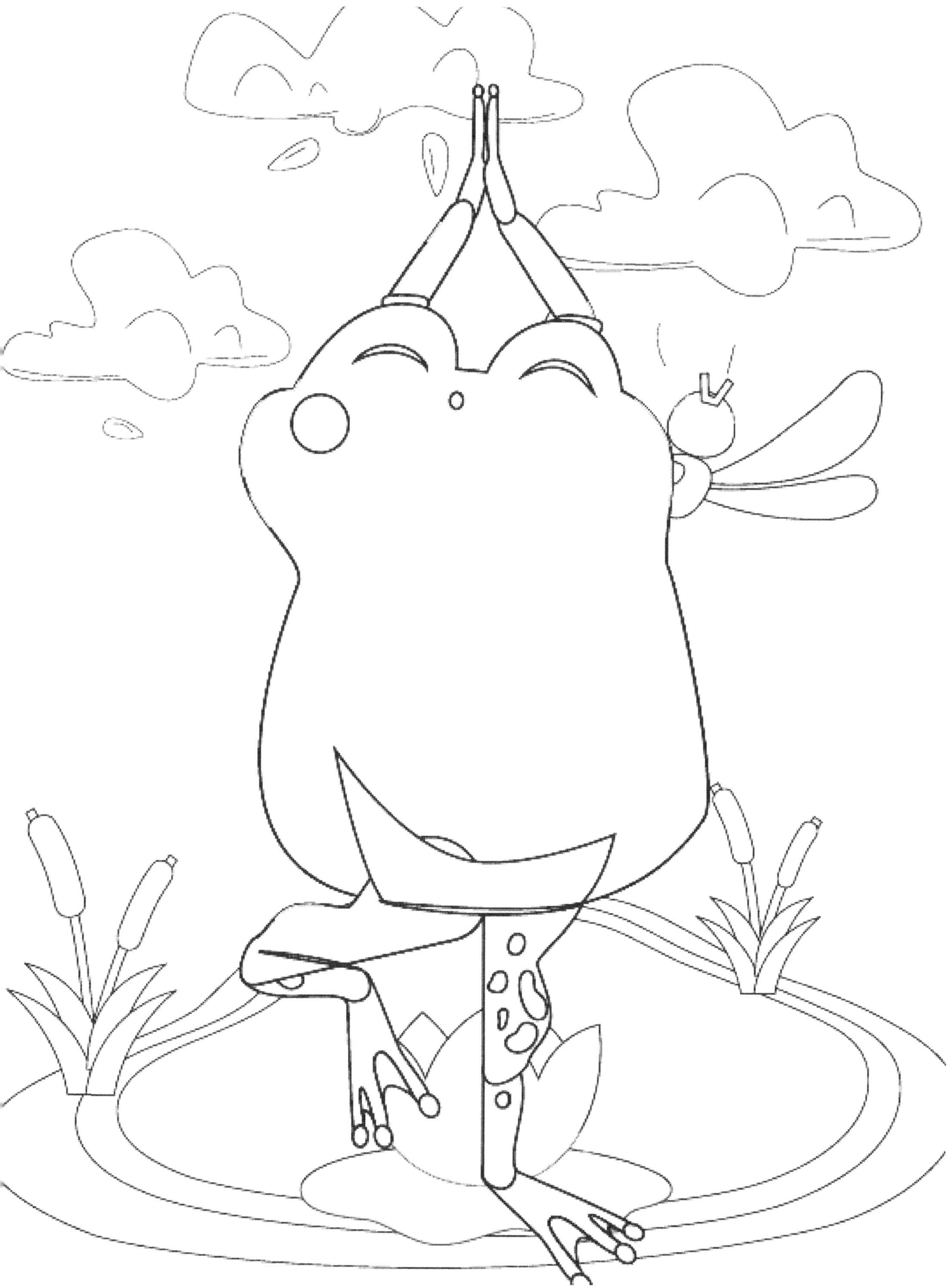

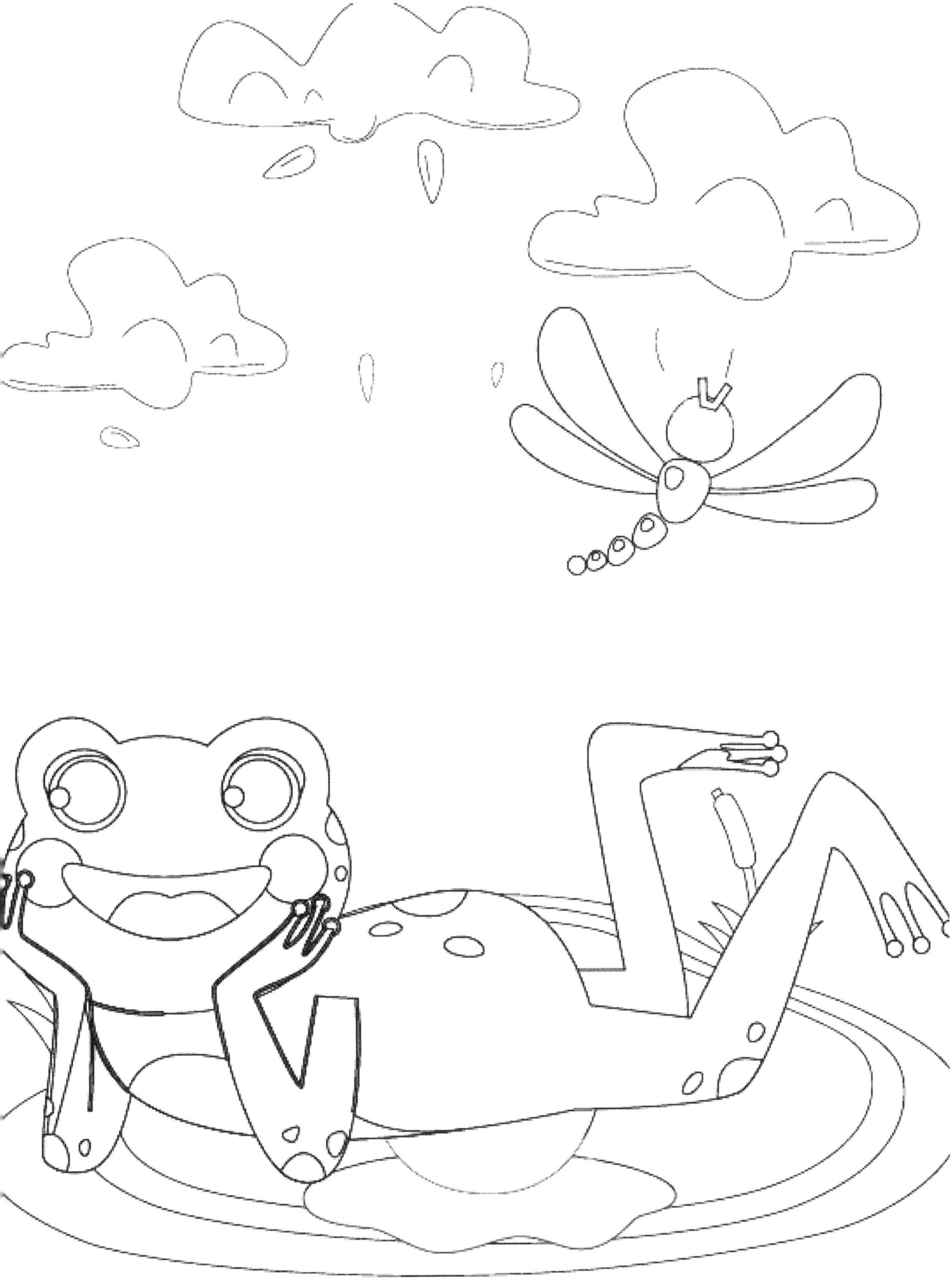

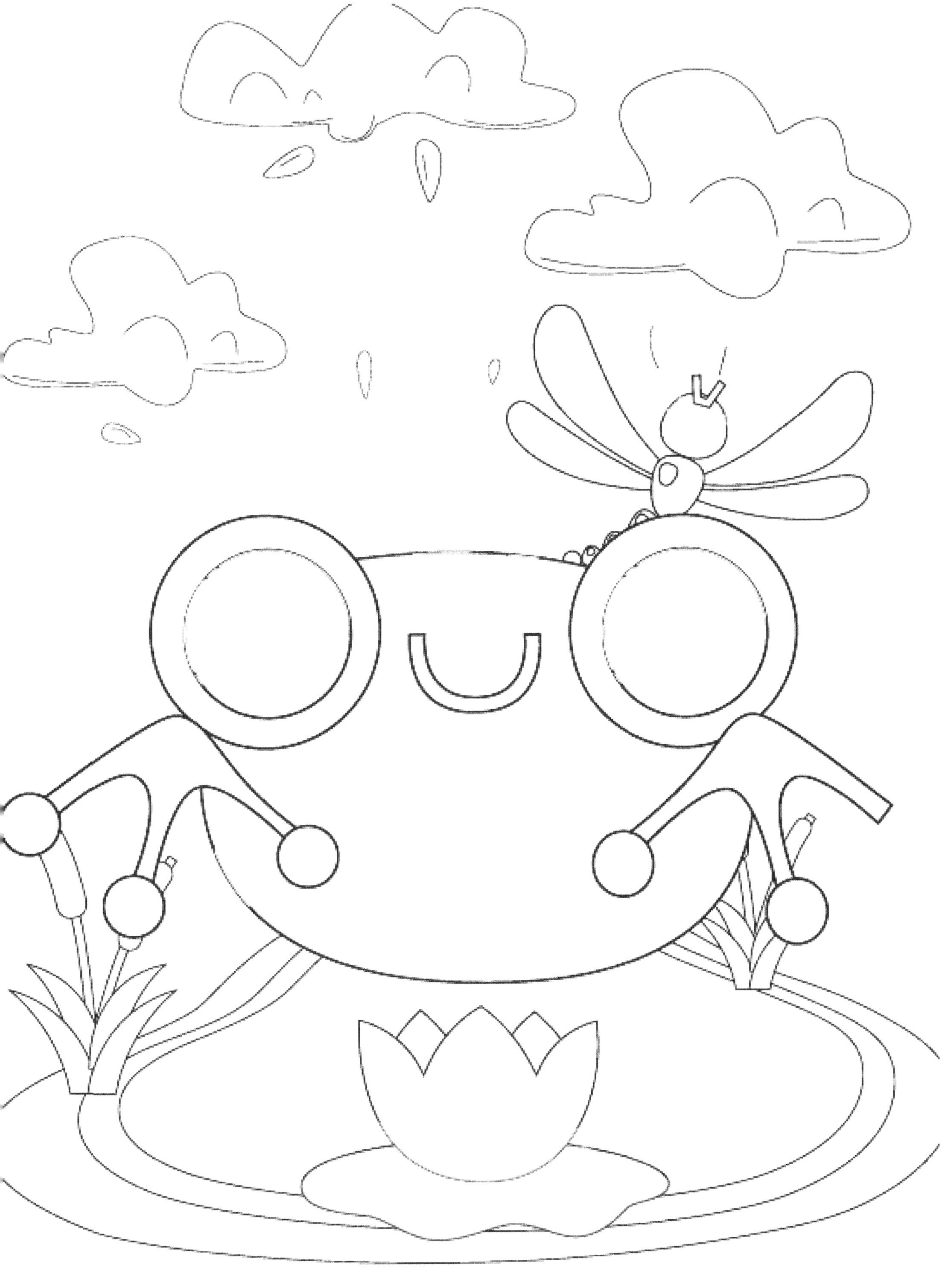

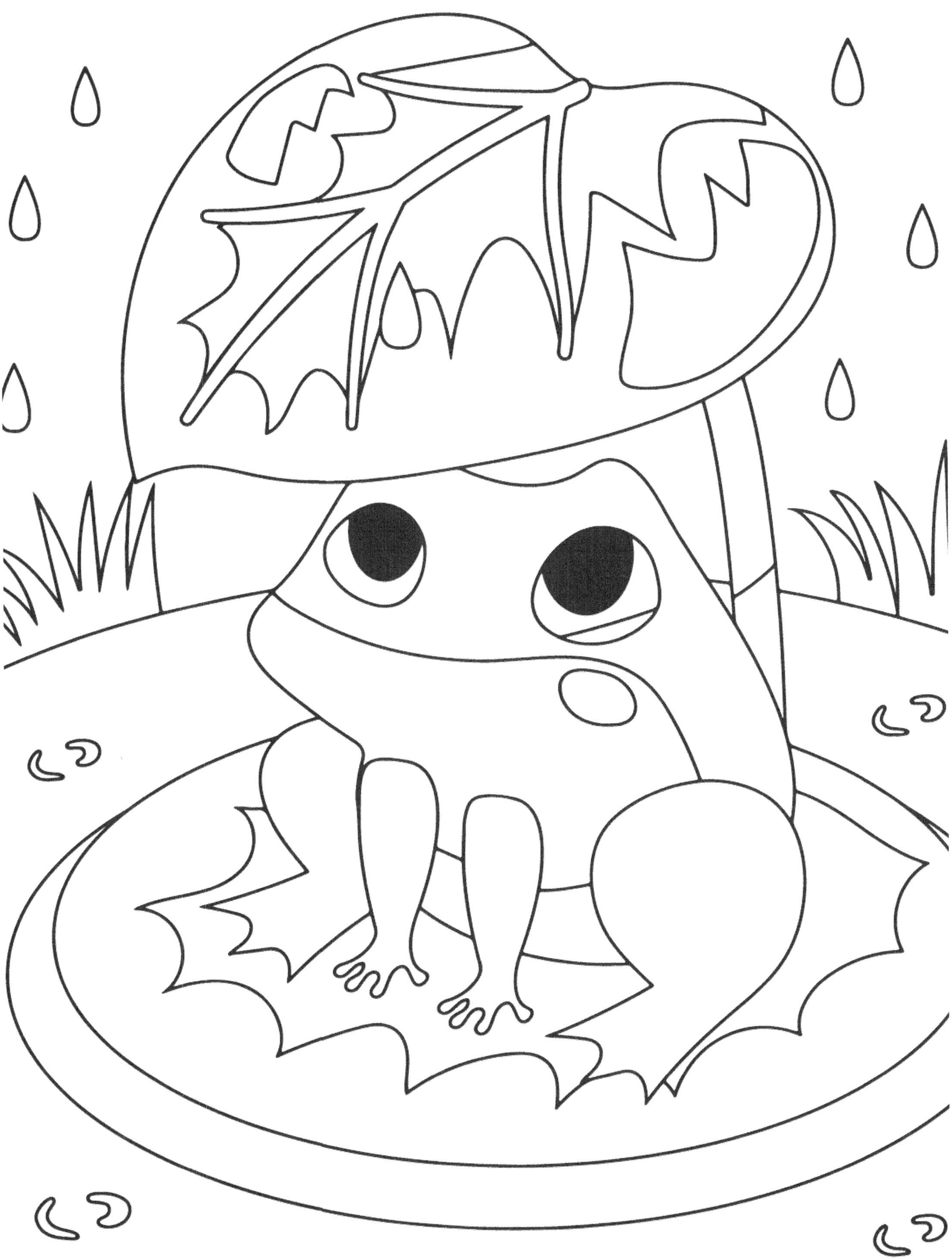

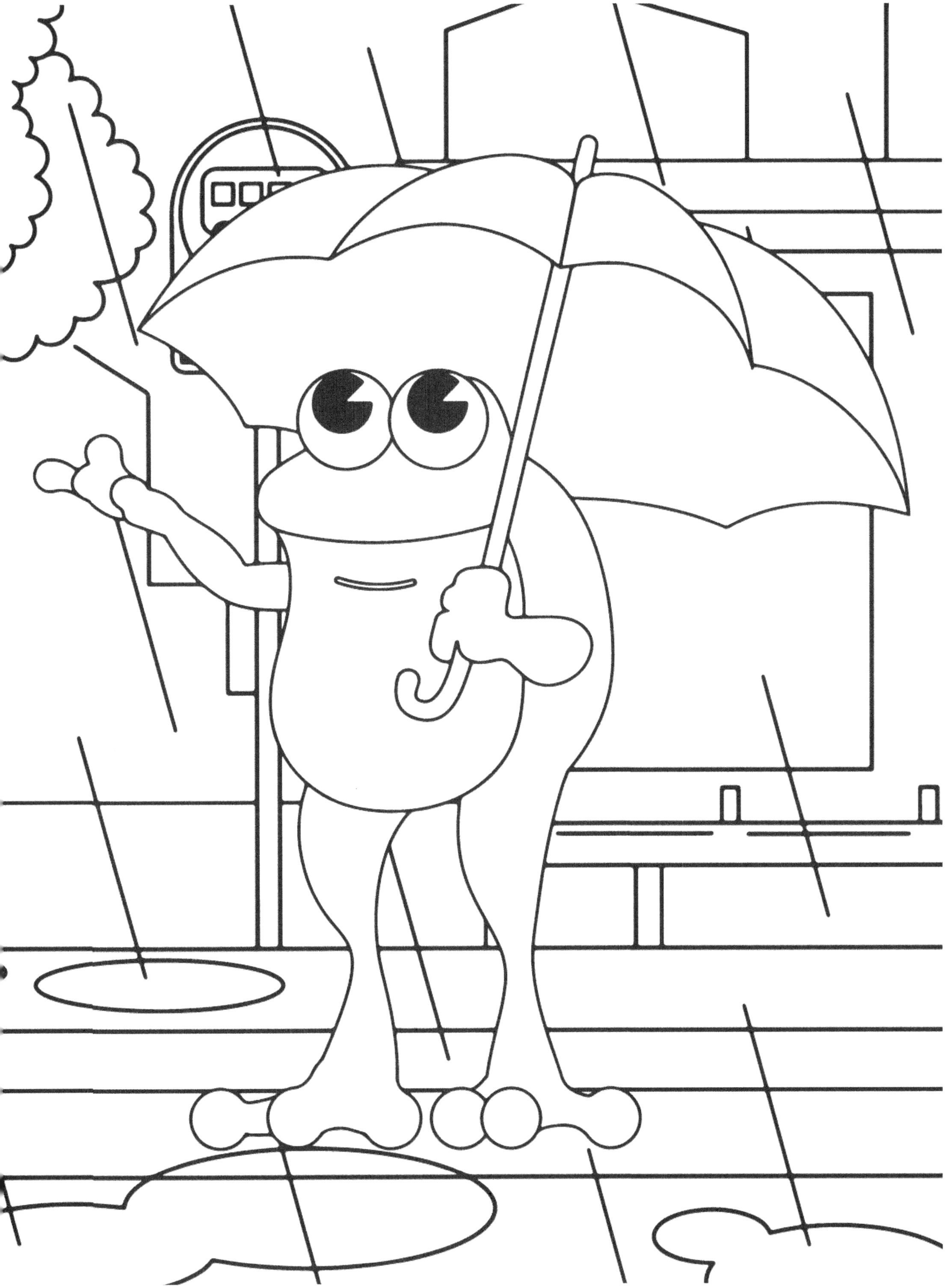

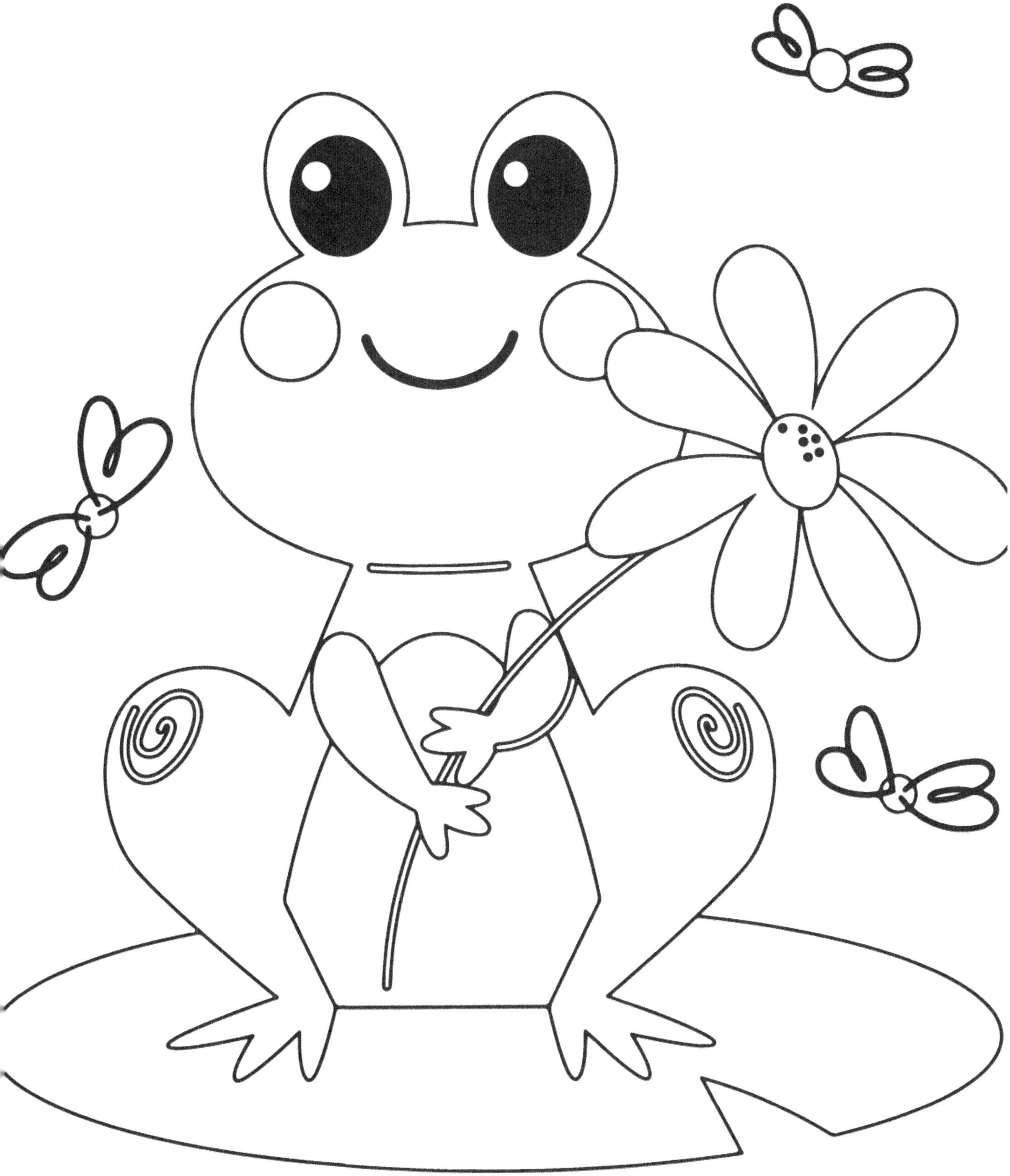

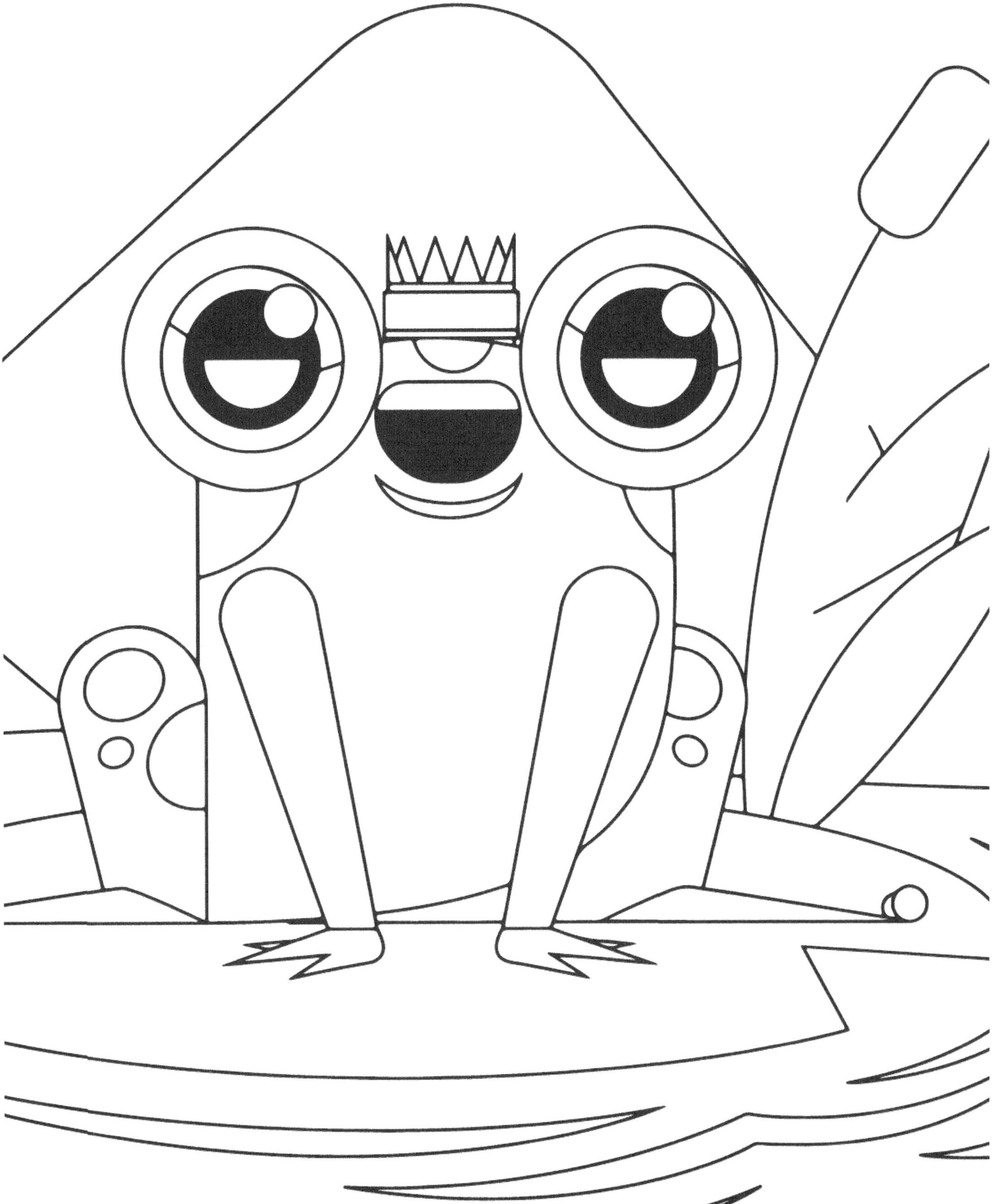

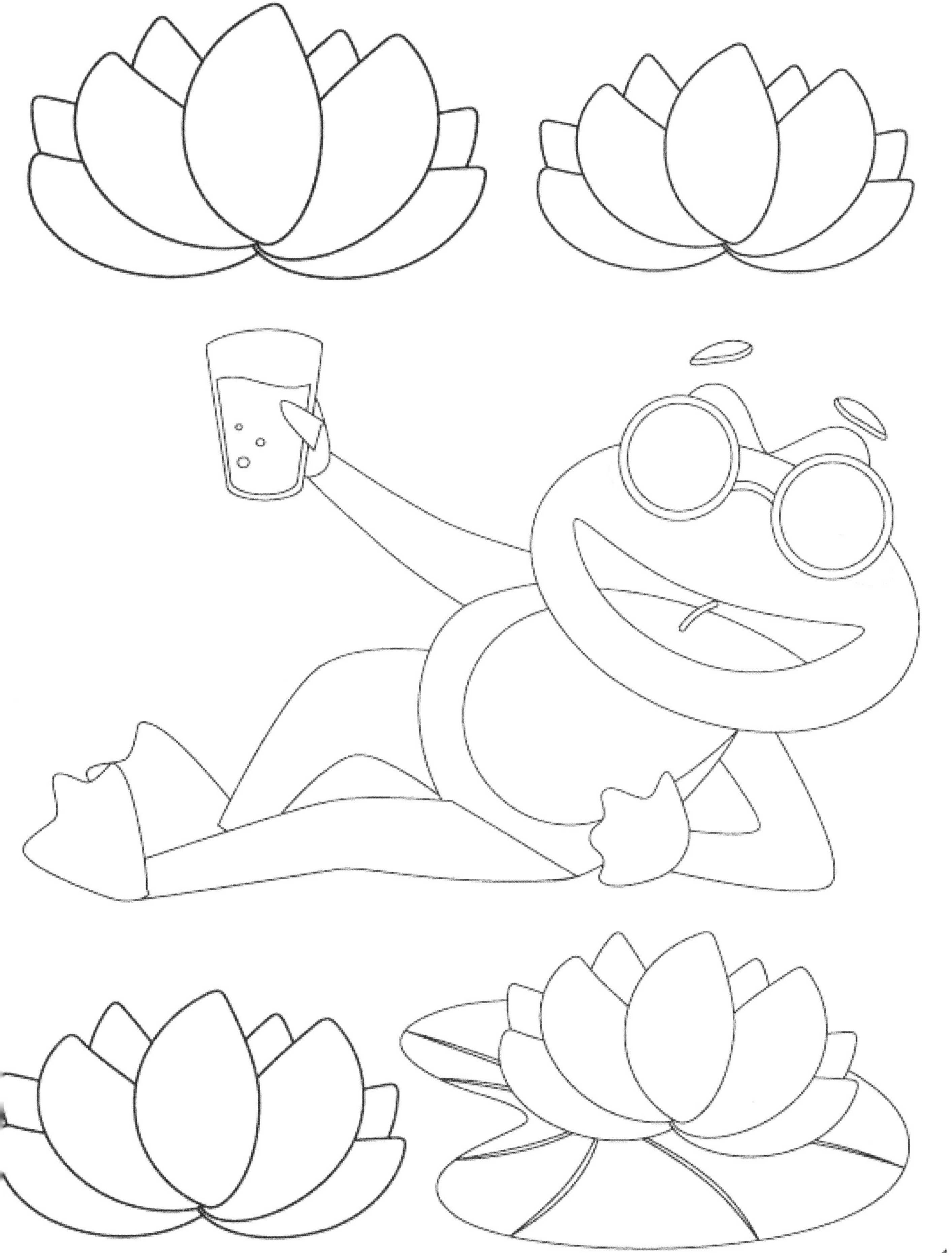

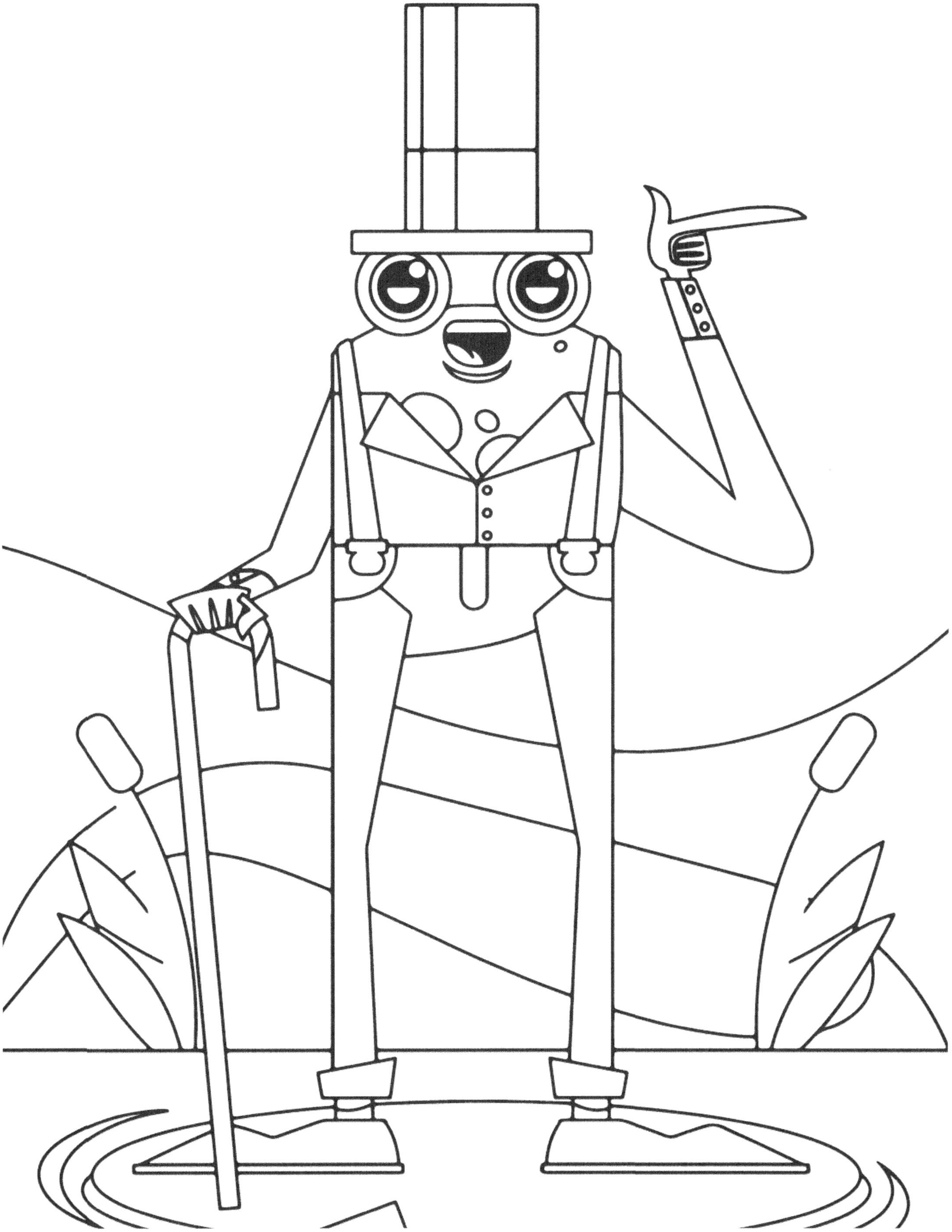

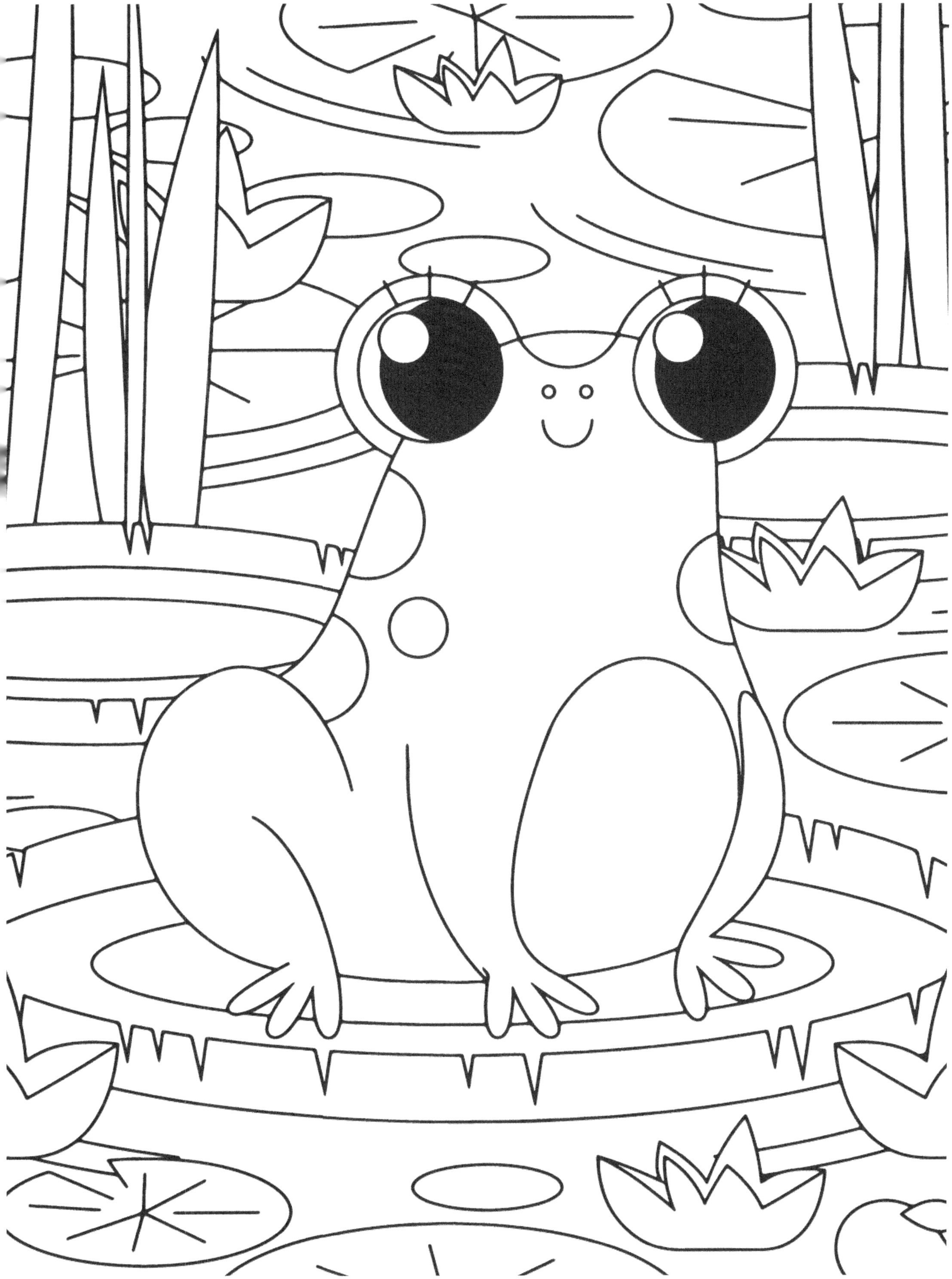

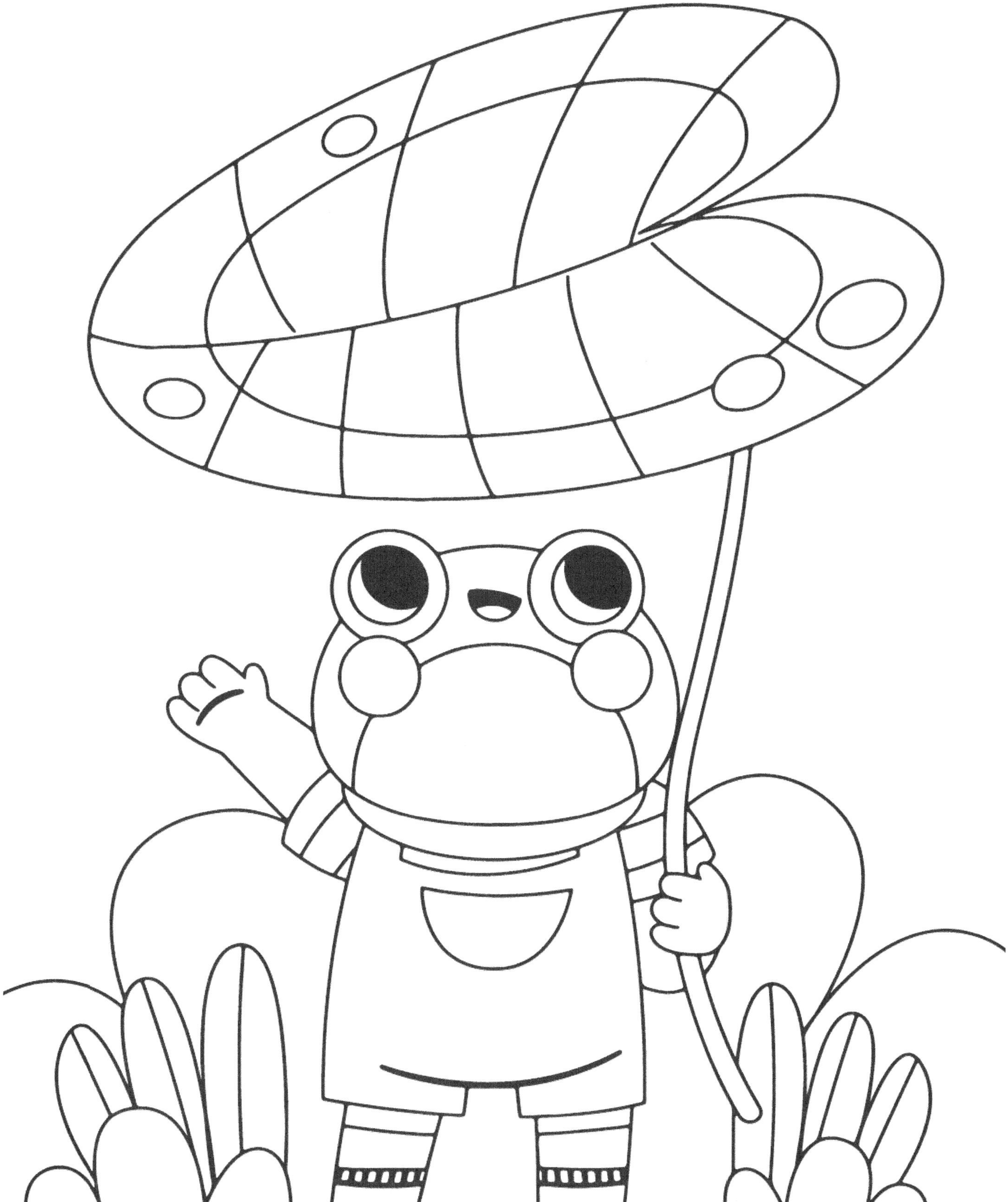

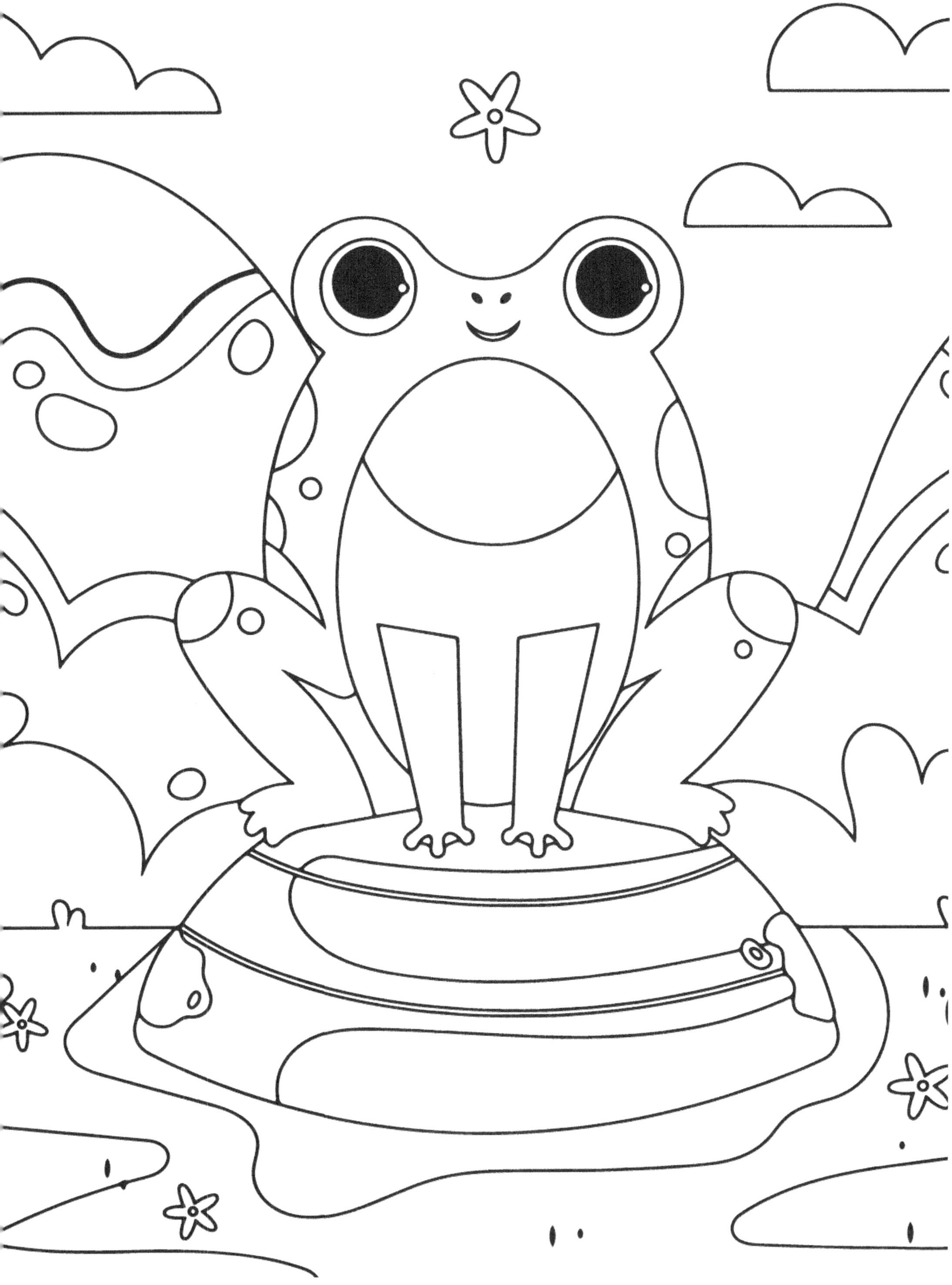

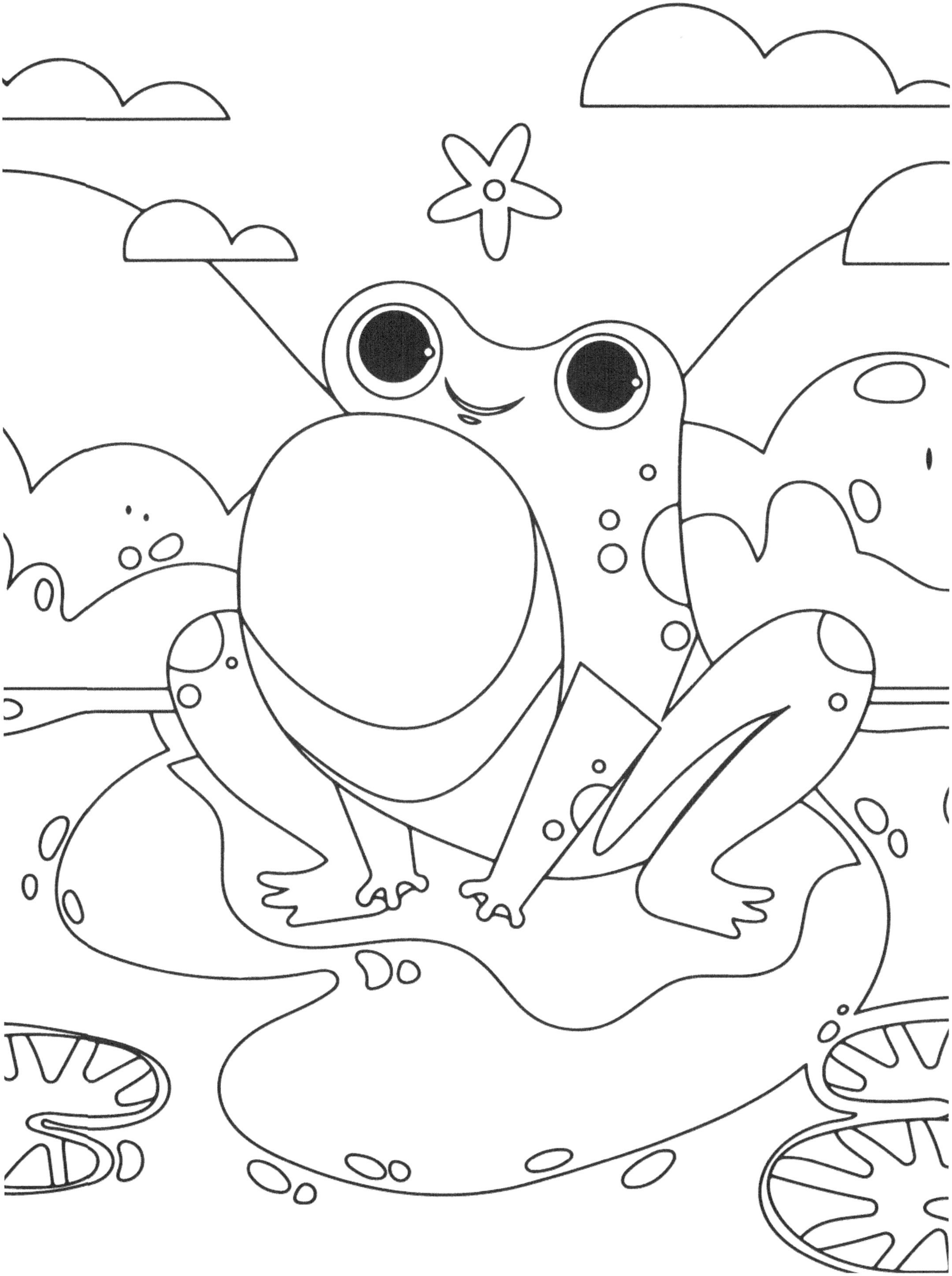

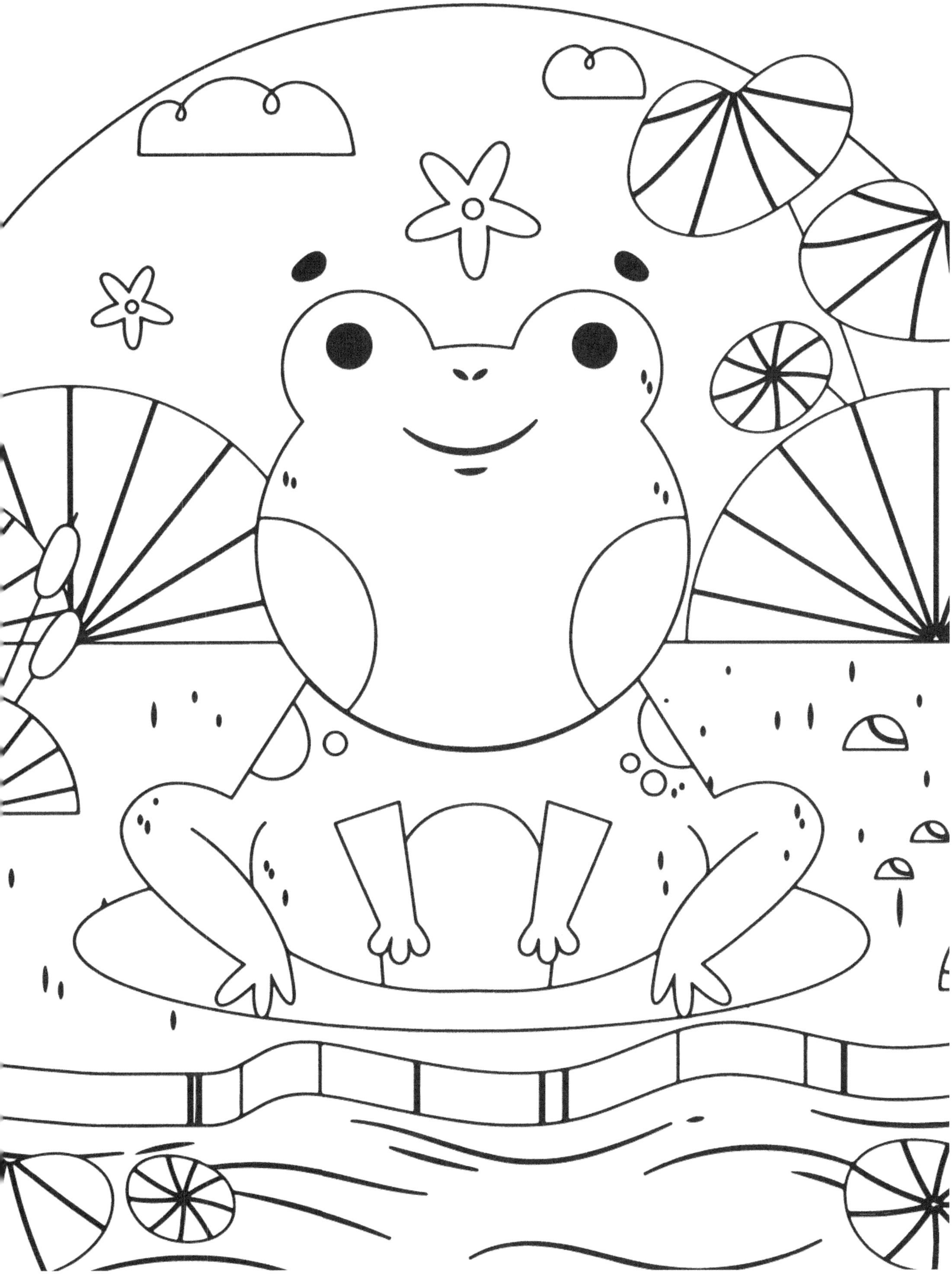

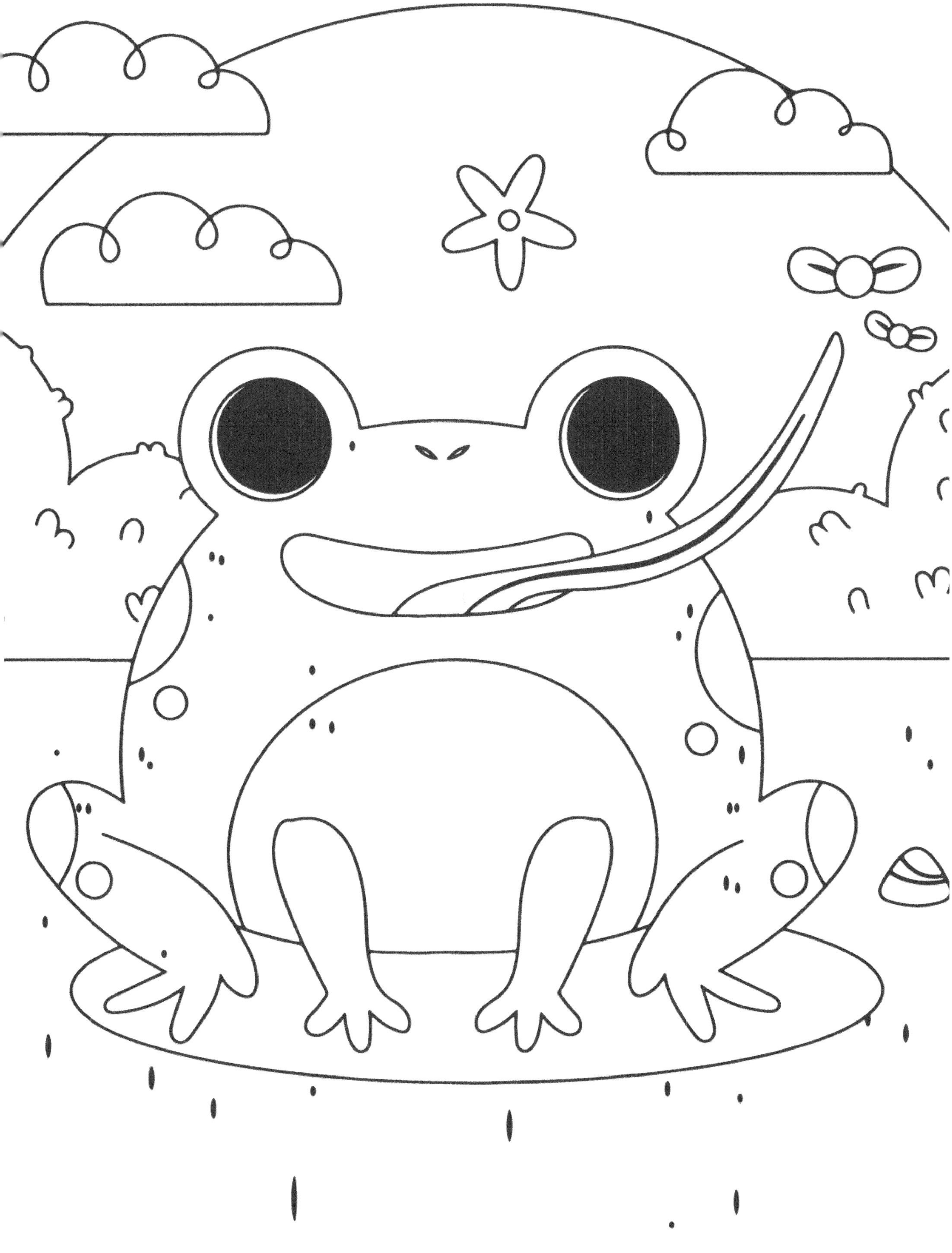

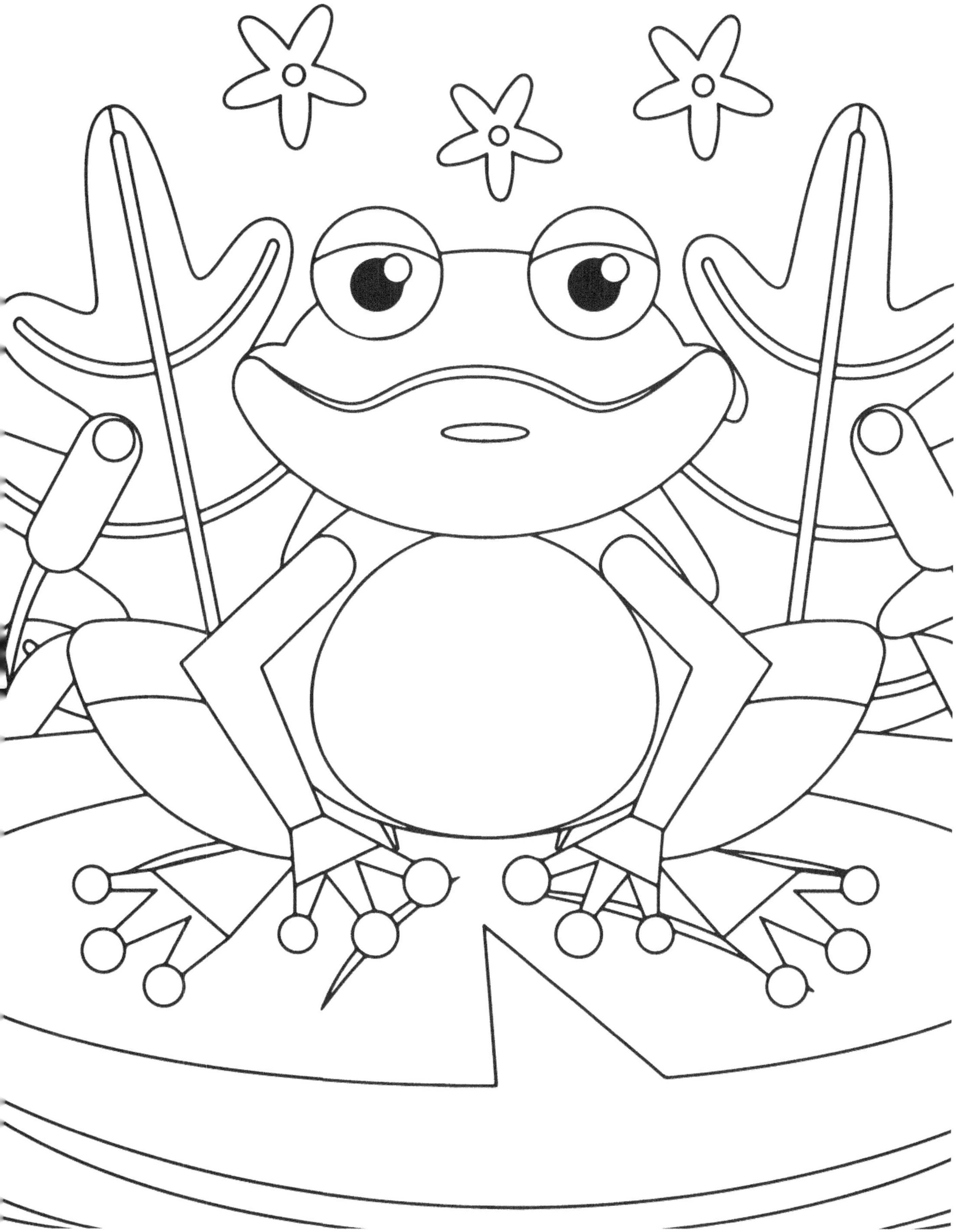

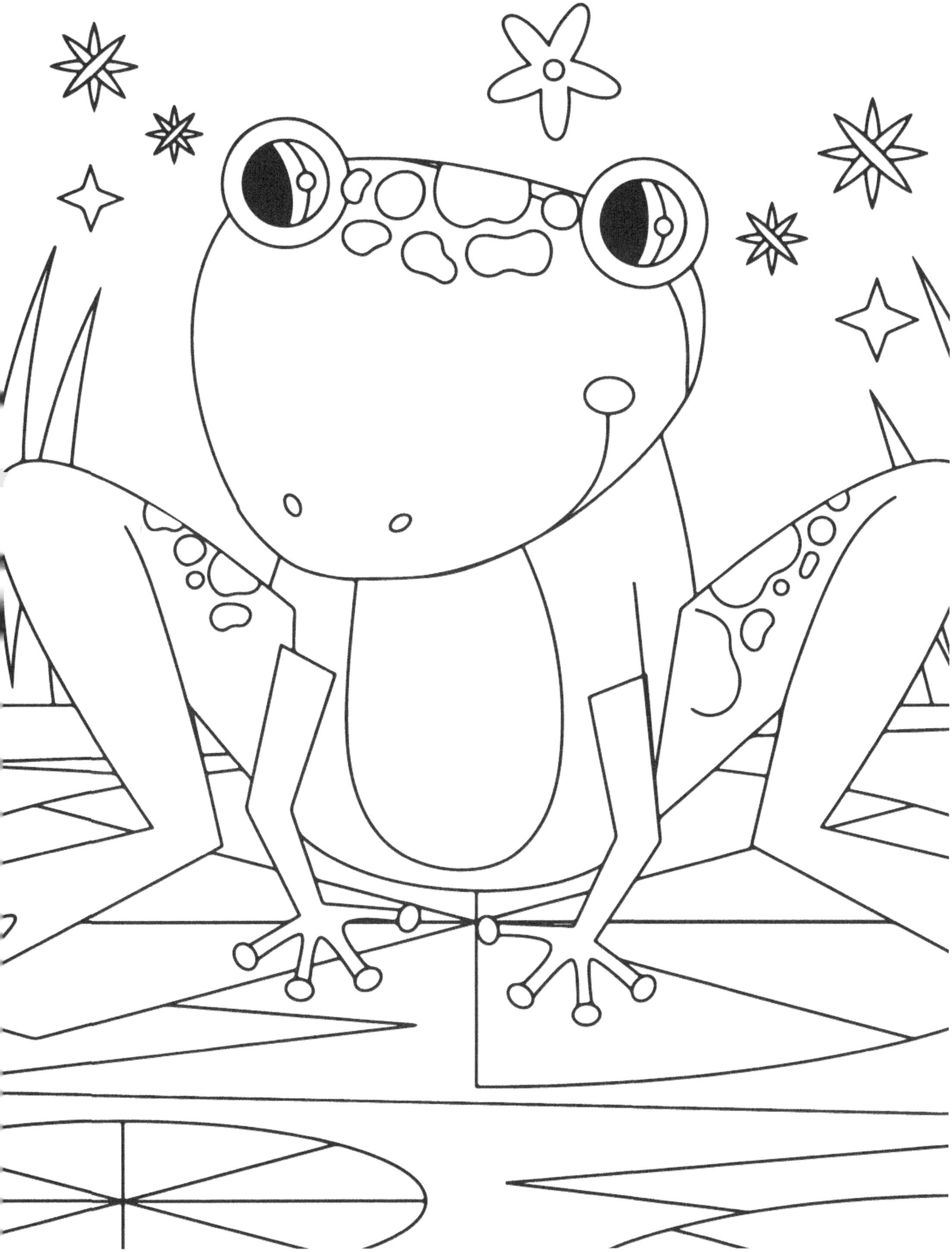

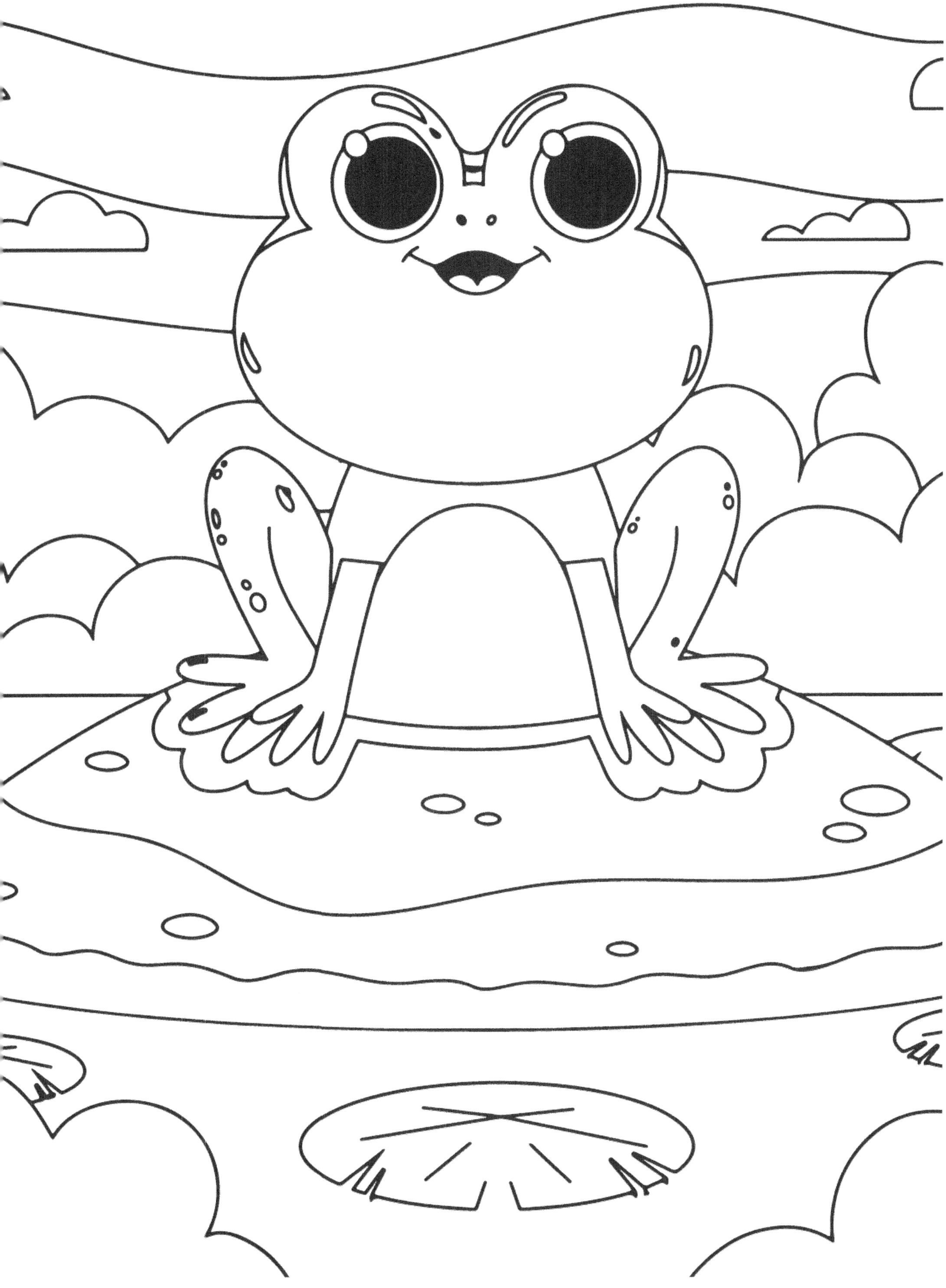

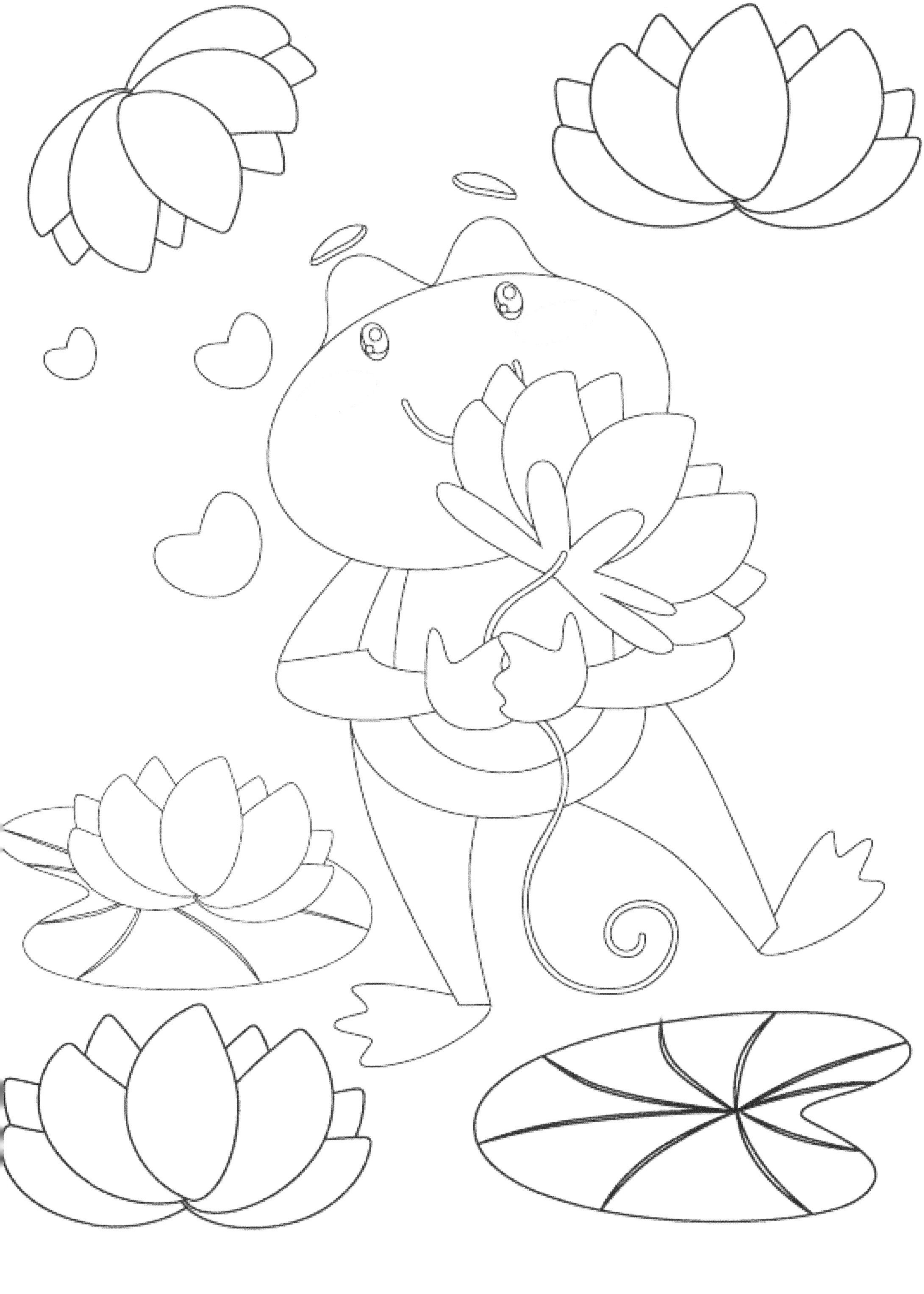

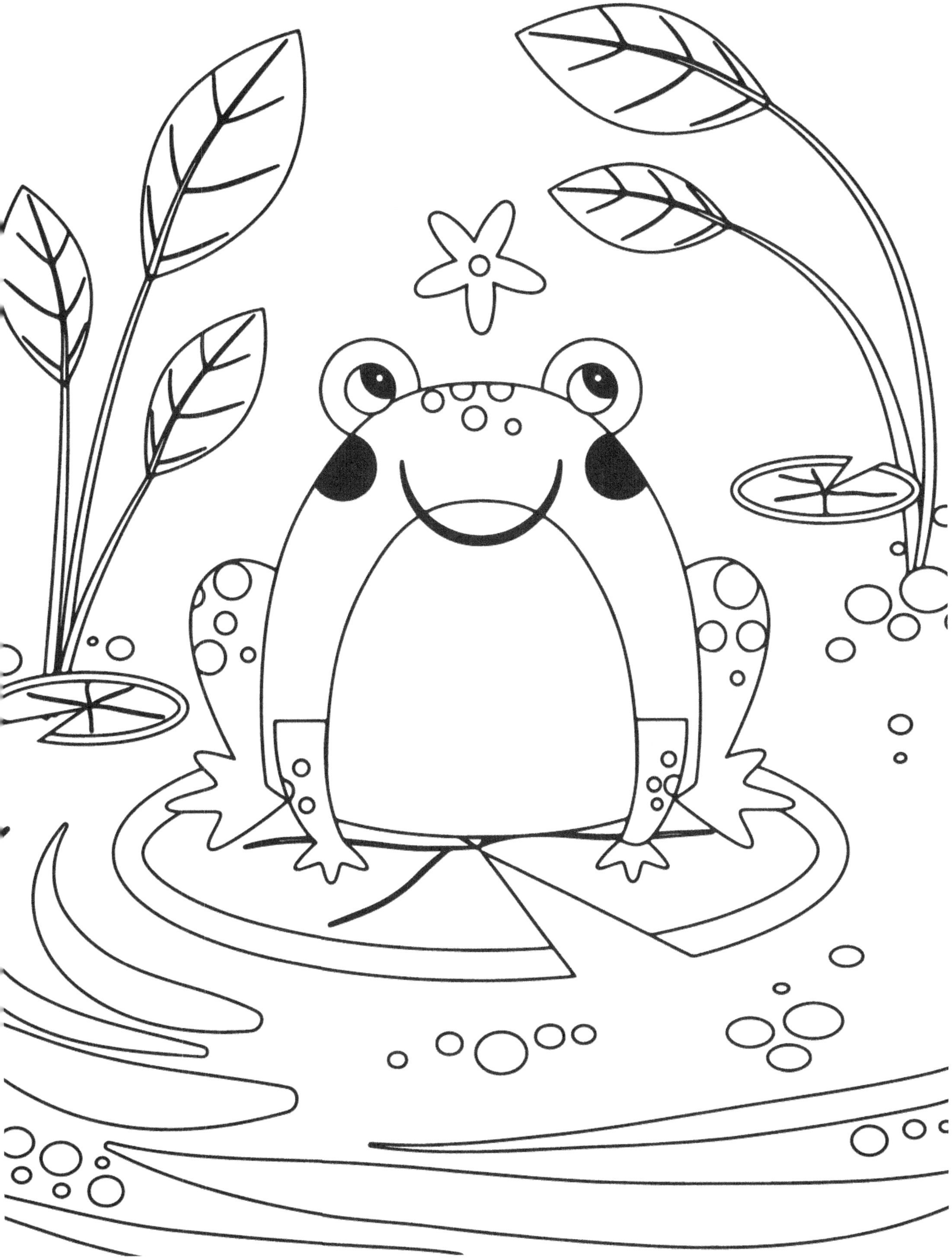

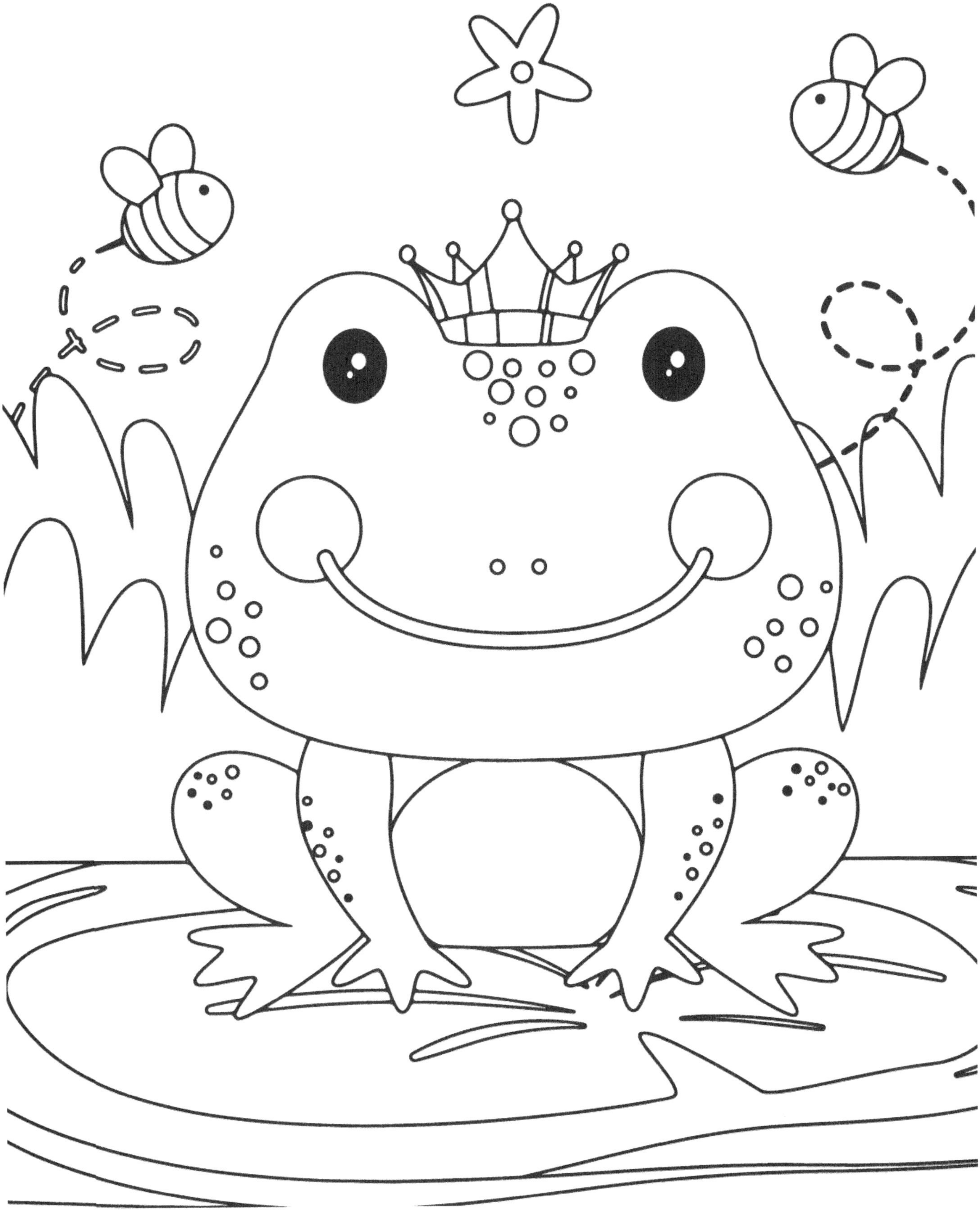

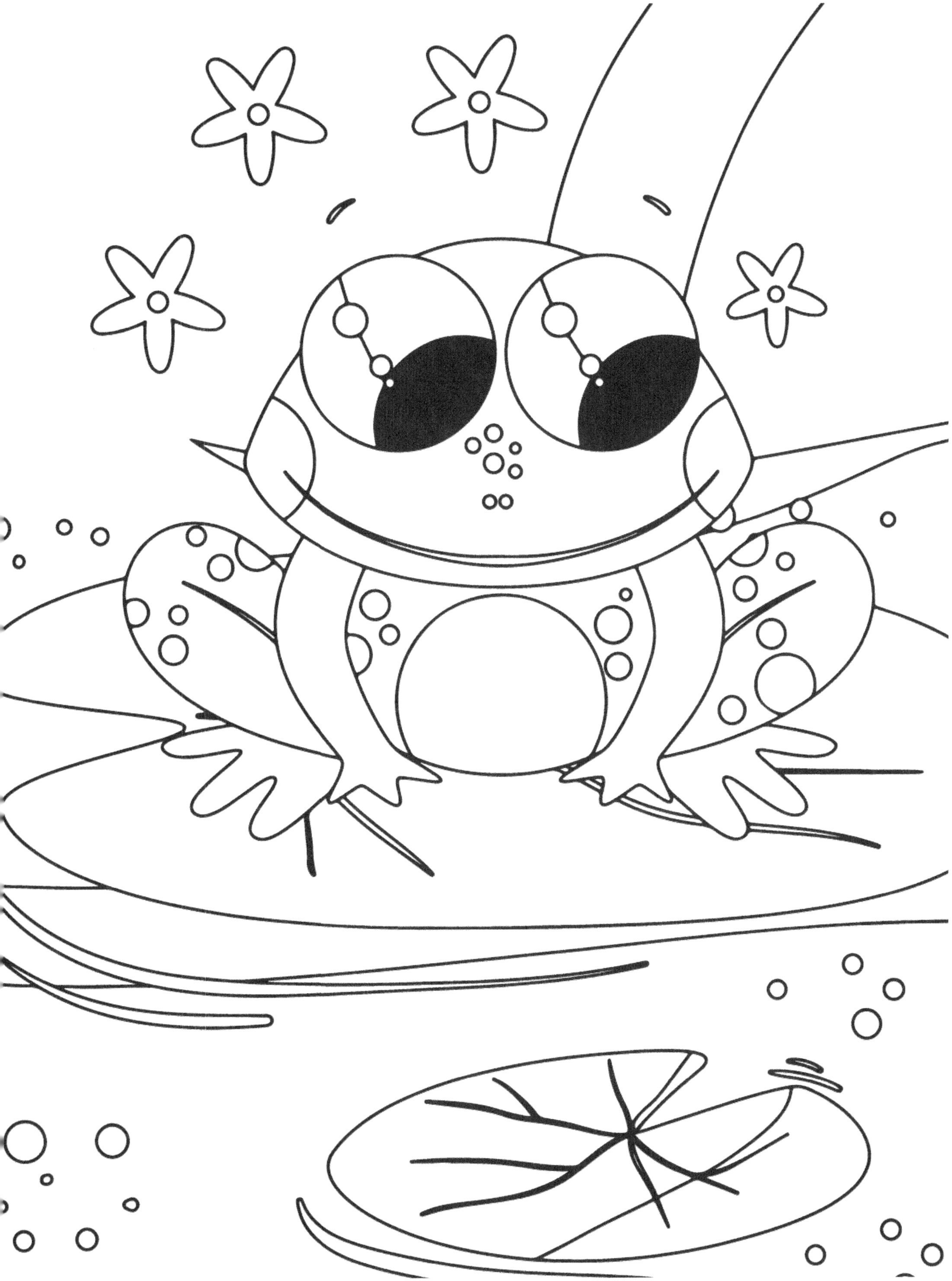

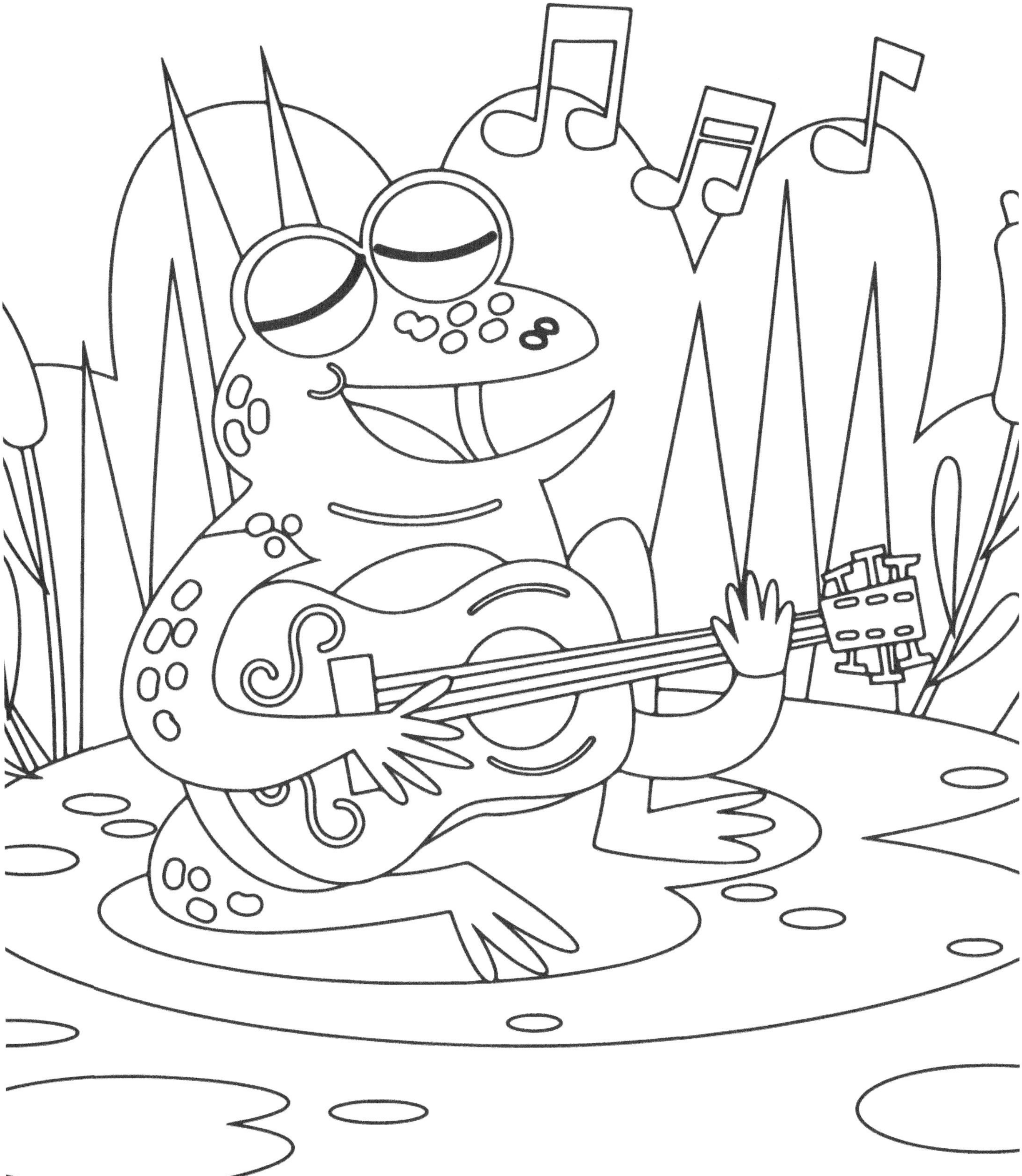

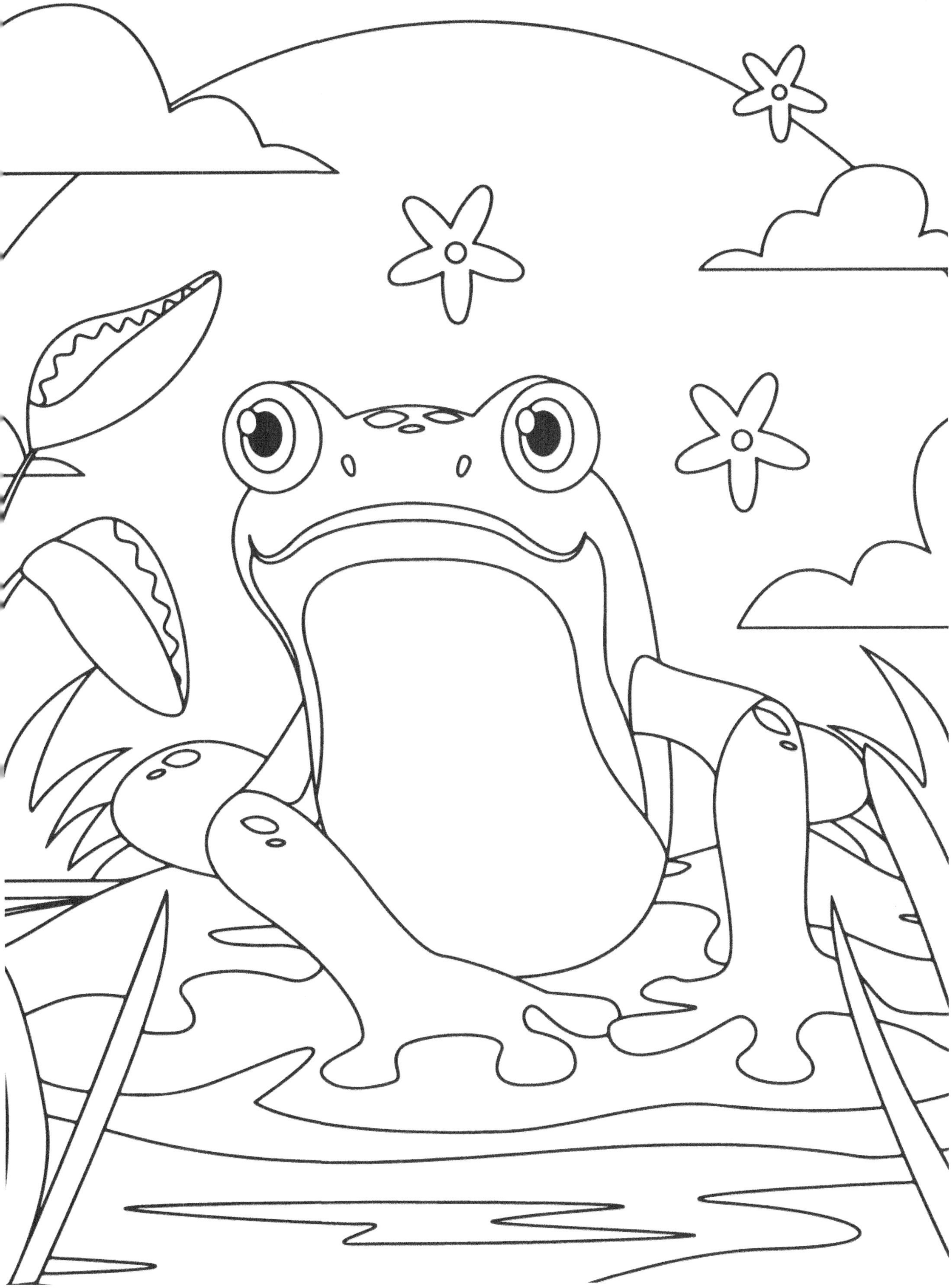

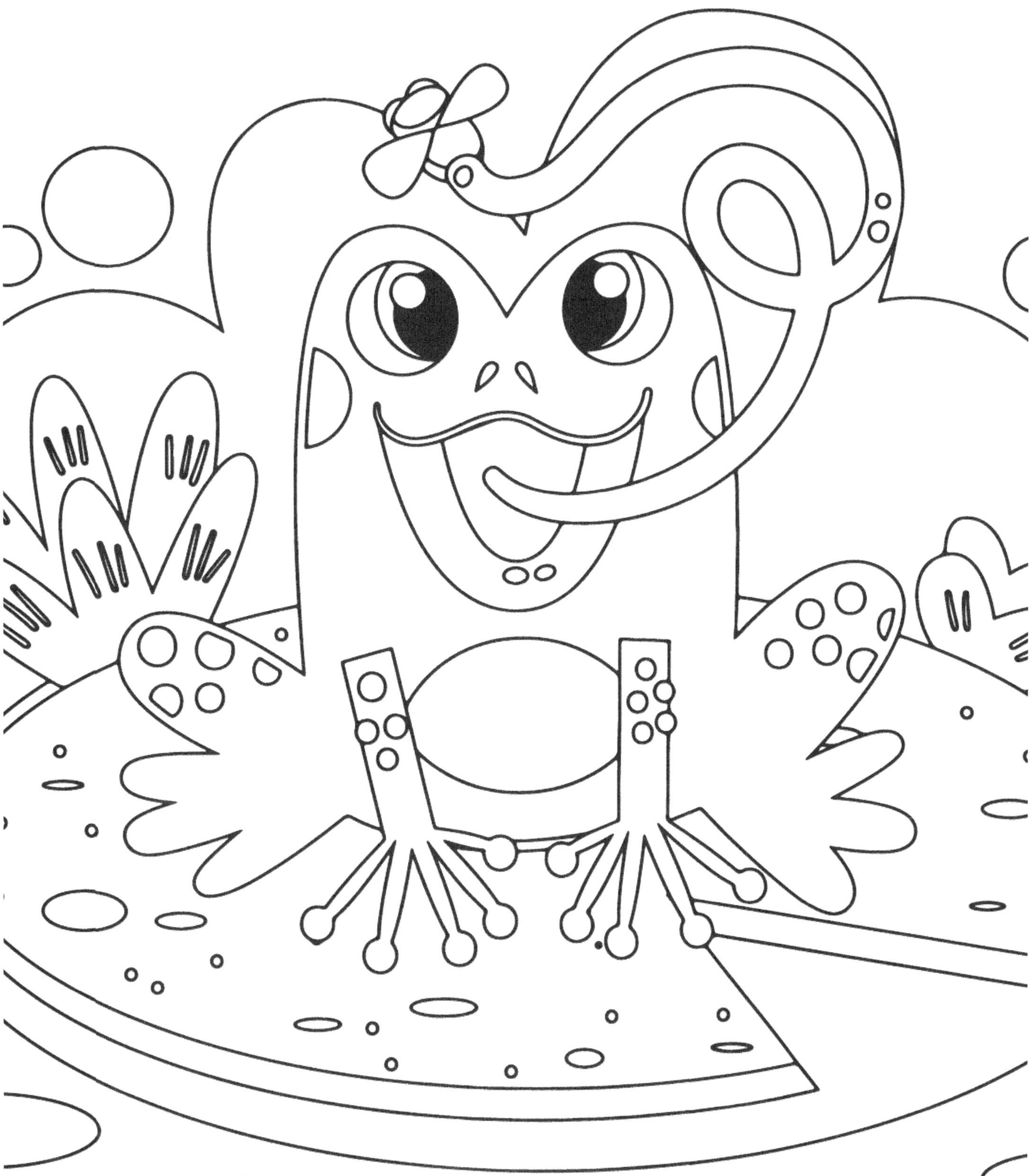

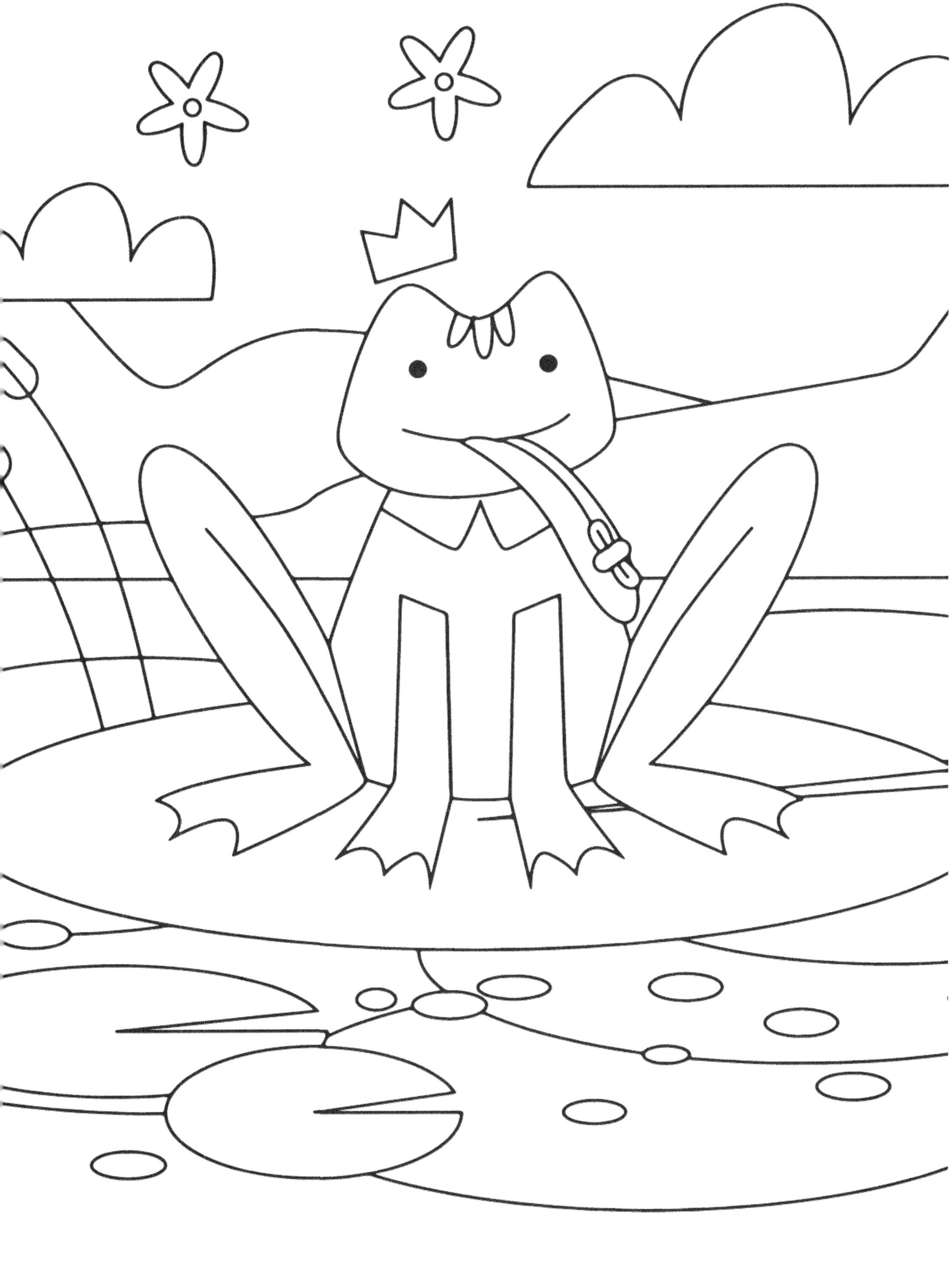

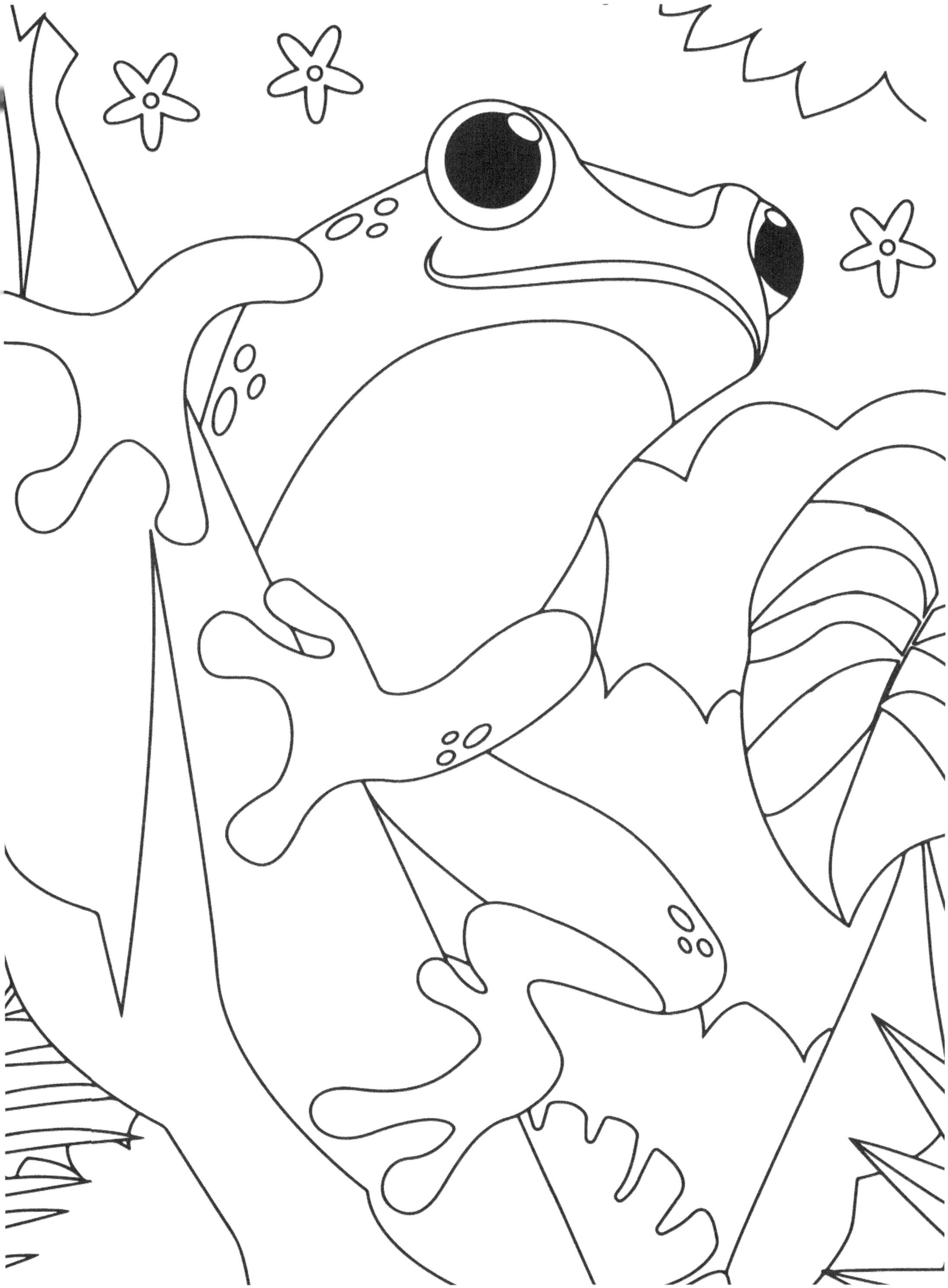

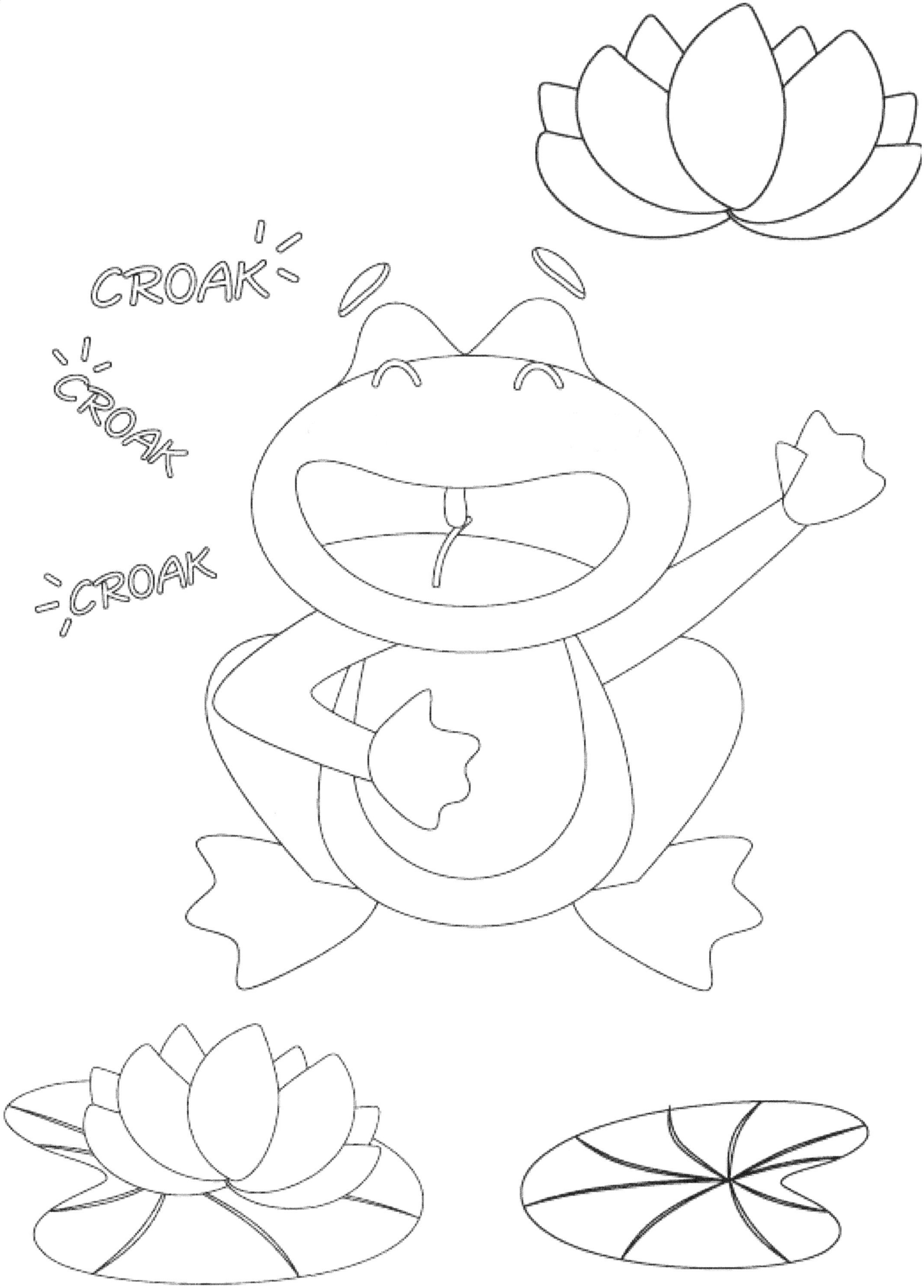
CROAK
CROAK
CROAK

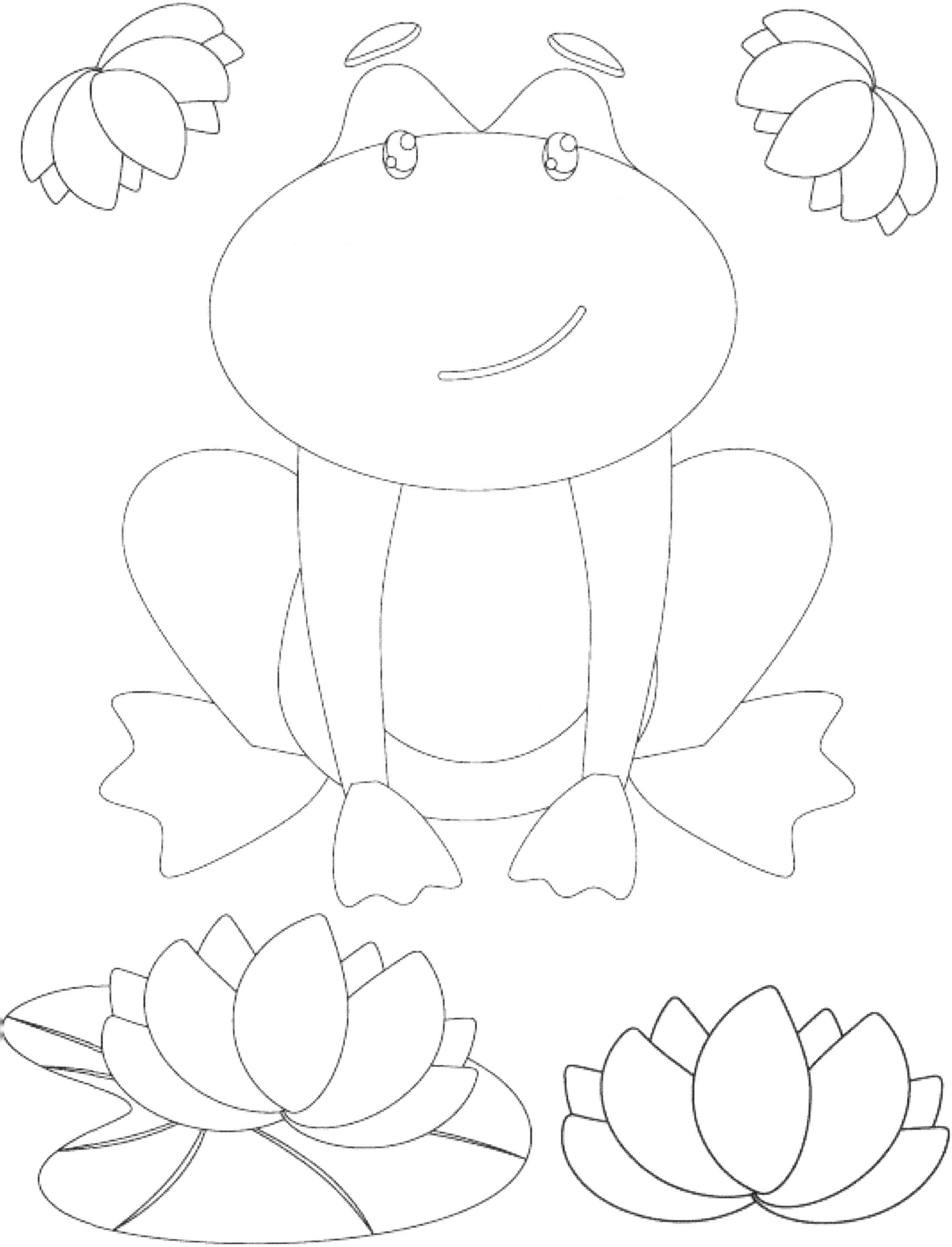

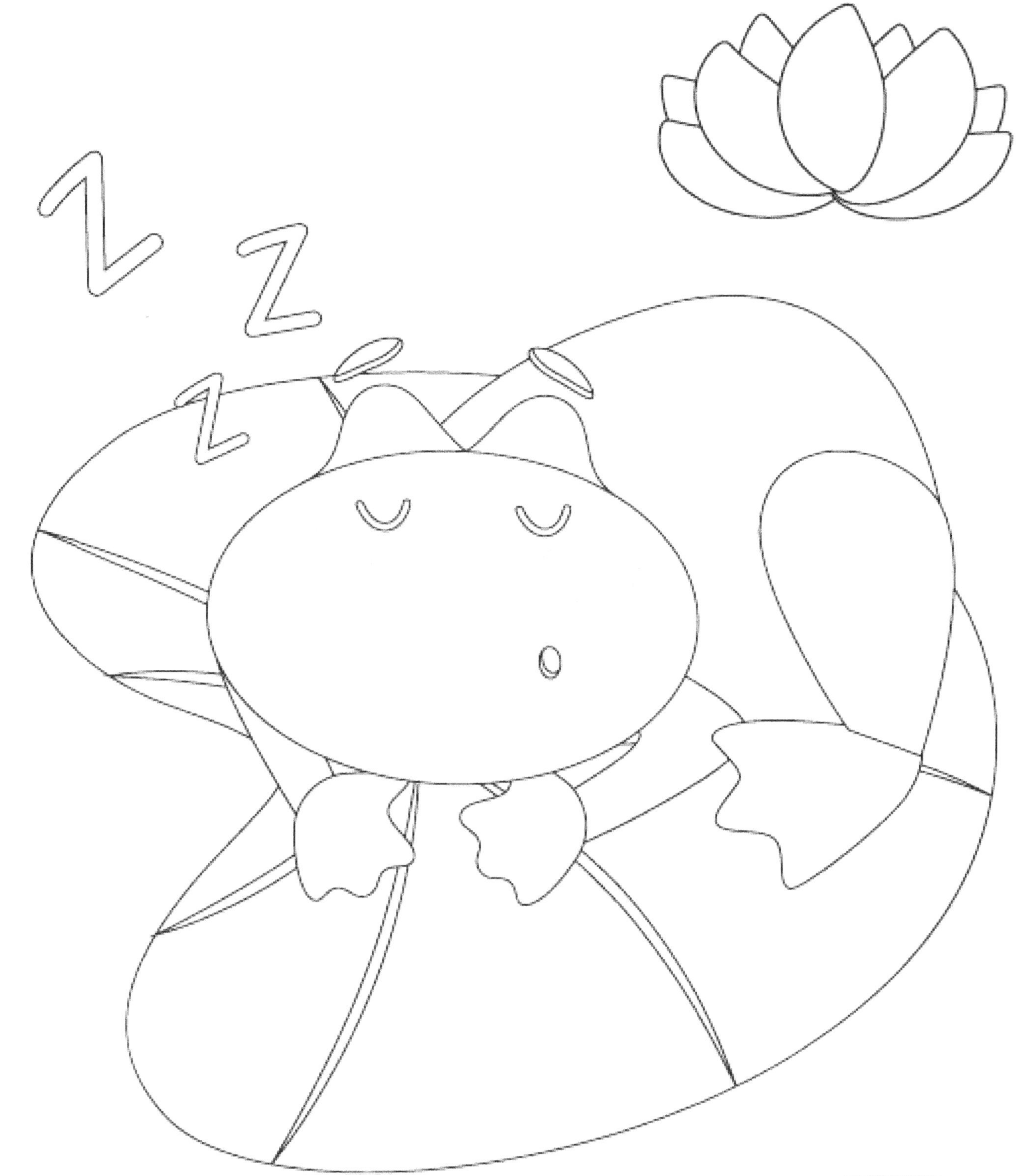
Z Z Z

Made in the USA
Monee, IL
15 March 2023

29926175R00057